LOST IN THE TRUTH

WHEN THE LIFE YOU KNEW NO LONGER FITS

SUSAN H HARRIS

THRESHOLD PRESS

Published by Threshold Press

Print ISBN: 979-8-9956980-0-5

Ebook ISBN: 979-8-9956980-1-2

First published 2026

susanhharris.com

*For every soul who has forgotten and remembered themselves
a thousand times along the way,
and for all who walk the unseen thresholds
between who they have been and who they are becoming.
May your path be met with truth, gentleness, and grace.*

CONTENTS

This book began long before I knew I was writing it.

It began in moments when something inside me shifted without explanation, when my body tightened for no clear reason, when tears arrived without a story, when the life I was living on the outside no longer matched what I was experiencing within. I didn't have language for those moments. I only knew that something was moving.

For a long time, I tried to understand these shifts with my mind. I tried to fix them, to name them, to move through them quickly. It took years to realize that what I was calling confusion was often the first sign of truth rising — and that feeling lost was not a mistake, but an entry point.

Some thresholds arrived quietly. Others arrived through loss, grief, and love that reshaped me. When my father developed dementia, I walked beside him as his familiar self slowly faded. As his world changed, old beliefs surfaced in me — about worth, receiving, money, and love. Parts of me felt young and ancient at the same time. What I did not understand then was that my own inner landscape was being rearranged alongside his.

Other thresholds came through places and moments that made no sense to my mind but left a clear imprint on my body and soul. In a cave in Nepal, where a guru had prayed for decades, I placed my hand on the stone where his handprint remained. Instead of silence, a simple song moved through me — carrying warmth and joy. It was unexpected and completely true. A reminder that the sacred does not exclude our humanity.

Over time, I began to recognize these moments not only in myself, but in the people who found their way to me. Again and again, I heard the same quiet questions: *Something is changing, but I don't know what. I don't feel like myself. I feel like I'm standing at the edge of something.*

They were not broken. They were standing in a threshold, a place where old ways no longer fit, and new ones had not yet formed.

One day, in the middle of my own unraveling, the title *Lost in the Truth* arrived. It named something I had been living for years: that the moments I felt most lost were often the moments I was closest to what was real. The truth was already present, moving through my body, my relationships, my grief, and my joy, even when I could not yet recognize it.

This book comes from that place.

It is not a map or a set of instructions. It is a companion for the in-between, for the moments when you can feel yourself changing but don't yet have words. You do not need to know where you are before you begin. You only need a willingness to stay.

If you are here, you are already being supported by more than you may realize, by your breath, your body, the ground beneath you, and the life that keeps moving through you. You don't have to walk this alone.

Thank you for walking this part of the path with me.

HOW TO WALK WITH THIS BOOK

An Orientation for the Journey Ahead

This book is not meant to be read quickly.

It is meant to be met.

You will find ideas here, yes — but more than that, you will find invitations:

to listen,

to breathe,

to pause,

to feel what is true in your body,

to notice what rises quietly as you read.

Some sections may speak directly to something you've been carrying for years.

Others may not land until later, when life brings you to a new threshold.

Both are part of the journey.

Here are a few ways to walk with this book so it supports you rather than overwhelms you.

Read Slowly

These pages are written to move you inward, not forward.

Allow space between sections.

Let what you read settle the way water clears after being stirred.

Let Your Body Participate

You may notice sensations as you read — tightening, softening, warmth, fatigue, a sigh, a shift in breath.

This is not distraction.

It is part of the experience.

Your body will recognize certain truths before your mind can name them.

Let it lead.

Notice What Resonates and What Resists

If something softens inside you, pay attention.

If something tightens or resists, pay attention.

Both are forms of recognition.

Both offer clues about where you are and where a threshold may be opening.

Pause When Needed

If you feel full or unsettled, put the book down.

Step outside.

Drink water.

Let your system recalibrate.

This is not a race.

It is a conversation.

You Don't Have to "Do" Anything

There are no steps to complete, no practices you must perform, no outcomes to reach.

Your only invitation is to stay with what arises as honestly as you can.

Truth does the rest.

Return When Life Calls You Back

Thresholds are cyclical.

So is becoming.

Each time you return to these pages, you will meet them as a different self.

Let the book meet you there.

Trust Your Own Rhythm

You may read a single paragraph and need days before continuing.

Or you may move through whole chapters because something in you is ready.

Your pace is part of your inner knowing.

Honor it.

Let This Book Be a Companion, Not a Solution

This book will not tell you who to become.

It will not fix you.

It will not give you certainty.

What it offers instead is language for what you've already been sensing,

companionship for the in-between,

and a way to recognize the thresholds you are already walking.

Let it sit beside you as you move into your own becoming.

INTRODUCTION — ENTERING THE TERRITORY OF TRUTH

There comes a moment in every person's life when the outer story no longer matches what is happening inside.

Sometimes it arrives suddenly.

Sometimes it approaches slowly, like a tide you can feel before you can see.

Sometimes it comes as restlessness.

Sometimes as loss.

Sometimes as a quiet knowing that refuses to be ignored.

These moments are often given many names, such as awakening, change, transformation, unraveling, but at their core, they are thresholds.

Thresholds are not dramatic.

They are intimate.

They live in the body before they live in the mind.

They show up as pressure, confusion, longing, fatigue, or a subtle sense that something in you is no longer willing to live the way it once did.

When this happens, many people assume something is wrong.

That they are stuck, failing, or unclear.

But what is often happening is simpler and more honest:

a deeper truth is beginning to rise.

This book is an invitation to stay with that movement rather than rush past it.

It will not tell you who to become.

It will not offer formulas or timelines.

It will not promise certainty before your path has revealed itself.

Instead, it asks for something quieter:

presence.

These pages are meant to be met gently and at your own pace.

This is not a book for the mind alone.

It is a book for the body, for the heart, for the places in you that feel change before you can explain it.

Wherever you are in your unfolding, at the beginning, in the middle, or in the quiet that follows, this book is meant to meet you there.

Not to lead you forward.

But to walk beside you as you listen.

Welcome to the threshold.

THRESHOLD PASSAGE

There are moments in life when nothing looks different on the outside, yet something inside you begins to shift without explanation.

You may feel tender for no clear reason.

Restless without direction.

Emotional without a story.

Your body tightens or softens in unfamiliar places.

Your breath changes.

Parts of you feel as though they are dissolving, while others are just beginning.

It can feel like losing your way, like stepping into an inner place without a map.

And yet, this is often where truth is closest.

Not the truth shaped by thought or effort, but the truth that rises quietly from within, long before it has words.

This book is for those moments.

For the thresholds you didn't choose, but find yourself standing in.

For the places where something is ending, even as something else gathers.

You don't need to understand what is happening yet.

You only need to notice.

To stay.

To breathe.

The rest will meet you as you walk.

THE MOMENT YOU KNOW
SOMETHING IS CHANGING

There's a moment, often small, almost forgettable, when you realize something inside you has shifted.

It doesn't announce itself.

It doesn't explain.

It doesn't arrive with clarity or direction.

It appears as a subtle unease, a tightening in the body, a sudden softness, or a quiet sense that who you were yesterday doesn't quite fit today.

Sometimes it comes as a sensation in the low belly, like the faint hum of something beginning. Other times it shows up as restlessness in the chest, a pressure behind the heart, or an emotion you can't name. There's no clear cause. Nothing obvious has happened. And yet, in that private way, the body tells the truth before the mind does; you know something is shifting.

You may try to ignore it.

You tell yourself you're tired, sensitive, hormonal, overthinking. You move through your routines, your work, your caretaking. You stay busy. You stay responsible. You stay in motion because sitting still would mean admitting you feel something rising that you can't yet explain.

But thresholds rarely arrive at convenient times.

They come while you're washing dishes, driving home, scrolling through your phone, or listening to someone talk about their day. They slip in through the cracks, through the sigh you didn't mean to release, through the way your body suddenly wants stillness, through the feeling that you're no longer fully inside your old life.

Sometimes the moment is louder.

I remember a day when my own body spoke with such clarity that I had no choice but to listen. I was sitting at home, not thinking about anything in particular, when a deep heaviness rose through my sacral region, dense, ancient, unmistakable. There was no story attached. No memory. No explanation. Just a surge of intensity that felt like something pressing from the inside.

My mind tried to explain it away.

But something quieter asked for my attention.

Moments like this can feel confusing to the mind and undeniable to the body. You might feel suddenly emotional, tender, reactive, tired, inspired, overwhelmed, or strangely spacious. You may feel like crying without knowing why or laughing at something insignificant. You may sense something loosening before you know what it is.

This chapter is about that moment.

The moment when something moves inside you before you understand it.

The moment when the old story loosens, and the new one hasn't formed.

The moment your body knows before your mind catches up.

If you are reading these words, it's possible you're in such a moment now.

Not the end of a chapter.

Not the beginning of a new one.

But the space in between.

You don't have to name it yet.

You don't have to understand it.

You only have to notice that something is moving.

Because this is where every threshold begins.

The Body Speaks Before the Mind Understands

Most people assume change begins with a decision, a moment of clarity, a realization, an insight.

But the kind of change that reshapes us from the inside out rarely begins that way.

It begins in the body.

Long before you can articulate what is shifting, your body starts to rearrange itself around something deeper. You feel it as tension, restlessness, tenderness, fatigue, or emotion without a clear story. You may notice yourself pulling inward or craving solitude. You may feel overstimulated by things that once felt neutral or unusually touched by small moments you can't explain.

Nothing is "wrong."

This is the body preparing.

Your nervous system senses when an old way of being is loosening.

Your tissues respond before your thoughts do.

Your instincts register movement long before there is language for it.

The mind, however, does not like not knowing.

So when the body speaks in sensation instead of explanation, the mind often rushes to interpret:

I'm overwhelmed.

I'm tired.

I'm regressing.

Something must be wrong.

But the body does not speak in conclusions.

It speaks in direction.

A tightening may simply be asking for attention.

Tears may be asking for space.

Fatigue may be asking for less effort.

Restlessness may be signaling that something no longer fits.

When these signals appear, the impulse is often to fix them, analyze them, or push past them. But thresholds ask for a different response.

Not analysis — presence.

Not effort — curiosity.

Not immediate understanding — companionship.

When the body begins to speak, it isn't asking for clarity.

It's asking to be met.

The question shifts from *What does this mean?*

to *Can I stay with myself here, even without answers?*

This simple staying begins to soften fear.

Because fear often arises not from change itself but from meeting sensation with resistance instead of care. When the body feels accompanied, it relaxes enough to reveal more.

Sometimes what comes is slow.

Sometimes it arrives in waves.

Sometimes it is emotion without a story.

Sometimes it is a quiet knowing that wasn't there before.

But it always begins the same way.

With a feeling.

The Quiet Dissolving — When What Was Familiar No Longer Fits

One of the most disorienting aspects of a threshold is that it doesn't begin with new clarity.

It begins with the quiet dissolving of what once felt familiar.

Not with a loud ending.

Not with a dramatic shift.

But with a subtle sense that something in your life, your identity, or your inner world is no longer quite true.

You may notice it first in small ways.

A conversation leaves you uneasy.

A routine that once felt grounding begins to feel heavy.

A relationship dynamic no longer fits the way it used to.

A habit loses its ability to soothe.

A boundary appears without explanation.

Nothing is obviously wrong.

And yet something feels different, not broken, but no longer aligned with who you are becoming.

This dissolving often carries a particular texture.

A subtle grief without a clear cause.

A loss of interest in patterns that once held you.

An impatience with what used to feel tolerable.

A sense of being half-in, half-out of your own life.

Because we are taught to value clarity over mystery, this phase is often misunderstood.

Many people assume something has gone wrong.

But dissolving is not collapsing.

It is softening.

The self you have been is loosening its grip, making room for something that has not yet taken shape.

You are between stories.

Not the one you have just lived.

Not the one you are about to live.

But the space where old truths loosen and new ones have not yet formed.

This phase asks for tenderness.

Not pushing.

Not self-critique.

Not pressure to "fix," "rise," or "figure it out."

Just presence.

Just the willingness to let what no longer fits soften without demanding what comes next.

Because every threshold carries a moment like this, a moment of feeling unmoored, not because you are lost, but because you are no longer who you were.

Even without words, your body knows this.

Your breath responds.

Your inner movements begin to shift.

The dissolving is not the end.

It is the doorway beginning to open.

The Inner Split — The Part That Knows and the Part That Fears

Every threshold carries more than one voice.

One whispers, *Something is calling me forward.*

Another whispers, *Please don't make me go.*

Both are true.

Both belong to you.

This inner split is not a sign of confusion.

It's a sign that you are standing at the edge of change.

There is a part of you that already senses the direction you're being pulled toward, even if you can't yet name it. This part feels the opening before your mind understands it. It recognizes the shift in your body. It knows something is beginning.

And there is also a part of you that tightens at the same moment. A part that remembers what change has cost before. A part that learned long ago to be careful, to brace, to hold on when things begin to move.

So when you stand at a threshold, these two parts meet.

One leans forward.

The other hesitates.

One feels expansive.

The other contracts.

One senses inevitability.

The other feels fear.

You may experience this as hesitation, doubt, or a push and pull inside yourself wanting change and resisting it at the same time. Longing for clarity while also needing safety.

This is not failure.

It is protection.

Thresholds awaken both what is emerging and what has been shaped by the past. You feel pulled forward because something in you recognizes what is forming. You feel held back because another part of you remembers what it means to survive uncertainty.

You are not doing anything wrong by feeling both.

Crossing a threshold does not require choosing one voice over the other.

It asks for something quieter.

To let the part that knows sit beside the part that fears.

To allow tenderness where there is tightening.

To stay present without forcing either side to disappear.

Because thresholds are not crossed through willpower or certainty.

They are crossed through relationship.

It is here, between knowing and fear, that something new begins to take shape.

When the Mind Reaches for Control

When you stand at a threshold, the mind almost always tries to take charge.

It asks questions.

It demands explanations.

It wants a plan, a direction, a guarantee.

It wants to know what is changing, why it's happening, how long it will last, and what you are supposed to do.

The mind believes that understanding is safety.

So when something begins to move inside you, something ancient, emotional, wordless, or instinctual, the mind rushes in to make sense of it. It gathers theories. It searches for answers. It tries to pull you back toward what is familiar, even if what is familiar no longer fits.

This isn't because your mind is wrong or unhelpful.

It's because it learned long ago that its job was to protect you.

But thresholds don't respond to thinking.

They unfold through sensations, emotions, impulses, and quiet knowings that don't arrive in straight lines. They move in waves, pauses, returns, and soft openings — often without warning, and rarely with clarity at the beginning.

So the mind does what it knows how to do.

It grabs the wheel.

You may notice yourself overthinking, analyzing, seeking signs, or trying to plan your way through something that won't hold still long enough to be explained. The harder you try to understand, the more disoriented you may feel.

This is often the moment people believe they are stuck.

But you're not stuck.

You're simply in a place the mind cannot navigate on its own.

Thresholds are not crossed through strategy or certainty. They are crossed through a deeper intelligence, one that lives in the body, the intuition, the nervous system, and the parts of you that are already responding to what is becoming.

When the mind is allowed to rest, even briefly, something else begins to speak.

A felt knowing.

A shift in the body.

A softening that wasn't there before.

Understanding will come, but not first.

It arrives later, as a reflection of what has already changed.

The First Real Sign — Presence Returning

There is a moment in every threshold when something shifts quietly, almost imperceptibly, and you begin to sense yourself again.

Not the old self.

Not yet the new one.

But the part of you that exists beneath both.

This moment does not arrive as insight.

It arrives as presence.

A soft awareness returning to your body.

A gentleness toward your own experience.

A subtle slowing of the mind's urgency.

A breath that lands a little deeper than the one before.

You might notice a calm that has no obvious reason.

A tenderness where there was tension.

A quiet in your chest.

The sensation of your feet on the ground, or the weight of your breath moving through you.

Nothing on the outside has changed.

And yet something in you has.

Presence is the moment the inner struggle loosens.

The part of you that fears no longer has to work so hard.

The part of you that knows doesn't need to push.

Your system stops bracing quite as tightly.

Your inner world becomes less divided.

This does not mean the threshold is complete.

It means you are becoming steady enough to stay.

Many people miss this moment because they expect change to announce itself as clarity, certainty, or a dramatic shift. But real change often begins quietly.

It begins as a soft return.

A willingness to remain.

A sense of being here again, even without answers.

Presence is not the resolution.

It is the doorway that makes the crossing possible.

And when it arrives, you may not recognize it as progress, only as a small relief, a little more space, a subtle sense of being less alone inside yourself.

That is enough.

It is how thresholds begin to carry you forward.

You Are Not Lost

There is a reason this phase feels disorienting.

A reason you don't feel like yourself.

A reason you can't explain what is happening, even to the people closest to you.

Something inside you is reorganizing.

Not to fix you.

Not to improve you.

But to loosen what no longer fits and make room for what is forming.

When your body tightens or softens, when emotion rises without a story, when presence comes and goes, something beneath the surface is shifting. An old way of being is giving way — even if you can't yet see what is taking its place.

You are not lost because you can't see the path.

You are simply no longer walking the old one.

And that can feel unsettling.

Your mind may not be able to follow yet.

Your emotions may not have language for this moment.

Your thoughts may search for certainty and find none.

But something else in you knows.

Your breath responds.

Your body adjusts.

Your inner movements continue, even without explanation.

You may not recognize this moment as part of your becoming.

You may not trust it yet.

You may feel unsure, tender, or overwhelmed.

That does not mean something has gone wrong.

It means you are inside a movement that has not finished revealing itself.

This is what it means to be *lost in the truth,* to be inside the change before you can name it, to be carried by something deeper than understanding, to be standing in the threshold without knowing what comes next.

Nothing is required of you here.

Nothing needs to be decided.

You are allowed to stay.

This is where the journey begins.

2

THE BODY'S MAP — WHERE CHANGE LIVES INSIDE YOU

Before you can understand where you are going, it helps to understand where change is already happening.

Thresholds do not live only in thought or emotion. They move first through the body, through sensation, impulse, tension, softening, and quiet shifts that arrive long before they make sense.

Most of us were not taught to listen here.

We learned to trust thought over sensation, clarity over presence, logic over instinct. We learned to move away from discomfort rather than stay with it. And so when change begins to stir inside the body, it often feels confusing or unsettling not because something is wrong, but because we don't yet know how to read what is happening.

The body is a map.

One many of us were never shown how to follow.

You may notice the beginning of a threshold as a tightening in the low belly, a heaviness in the chest, a pressure behind the heart, or a quiet restlessness that has no clear cause. You might feel drawn inward, unexpectedly tender, or aware of places in yourself that suddenly feel more alive.

These sensations are not random.

They are information.

They point to where old stories are loosening, where the nervous system is responding, and where something new is beginning to orient itself. Different areas of the body carry different kinds of memory and intelligence, and thresholds activate these places not to overwhelm you, but to guide you.

This chapter is about learning to recognize that guidance.

Not as a technique or spiritual exercise, but as a way of understanding yourself more honestly and more gently. A way of noticing where change is speaking from, so you don't have to fight it or rush past it.

Thresholds require inner companionship.

And companionship begins by knowing where change is asking to be met.

The Low Belly — Where Safety and Receiving First Speak

For many people, one of the earliest places to respond during a threshold, is the low belly — the sacral region.

This is the part of you that responds before the mind forms a question and before the heart makes sense of what it feels. It is instinctive, immediate, and deeply honest. When something begins to shift inside you, the low belly often knows first.

Even when you can't name what is happening, this place responds.

The low belly is closely tied to your earliest experiences of safety and belonging. It carries memory that predates language, impressions formed long before you learned how to explain yourself or manage your feelings. Because of this, when deeper layers of truth begin to move, they rise through sensation rather than understanding.

You may feel this as heaviness or tightening, warmth or fluttering, numbness or pressure, or an unexpected emptiness. You may not know what is changing yet, but something is.

This region also holds your relationship to receiving.

Not just receiving love or support, but receiving life itself, nourishment, rest, possibility, expansion, ease. When you approach a threshold, when something new is trying to enter your life, this part of the body quietly asks: *Is it safe to let this in?*

If the answer is uncertain, the body doesn't punish you.

It protects you.

The low belly tightens not to stop you, but to assess what is being asked. It remembers what it once took to survive. It wants to know whether the next step can be taken without abandoning what still needs care.

This is why thresholds often feel intense here.

Every threshold involves a shift in what you allow yourself to receive, what you believe is possible, what you believe you are allowed to have, and who you believe you can become. The low belly senses this long before the mind catches up.

What you feel here is not danger.

It is negotiation.

Old stories loosening.

Younger parts stirring.

Protection softening.

Truth beginning to rise.

This is the place where instinct and becoming meet.

And when fear and possibility are both present, it can feel alive and unsettling at the same time.

Your body is not resisting the threshold.

It is figuring out how to move forward with honesty, safety, and care.

The Solar Plexus — Where Identity and Shame Rise to the Surface

If the low belly holds your sense of safety, the solar plexus, the space just below the ribs, holds your sense of self.

This is where you learned who you needed to be in order to belong. How much of yourself was safe to show. When to take up space and when to shrink back. How to adapt, protect, perform, or hold yourself together in the face of what felt uncertain.

The solar plexus carries identity, not the deepest truth of who you are, but the version shaped by early experience, culture, expectation, and survival. Because of this, thresholds often disrupt this area quickly and noticeably.

When something new begins to emerge, this center feels the pressure of becoming more honest.

You may notice tension, heat, fluttering, nausea, emotional surges, or a vague sense of *I don't know who I am right now.* This is not chaos, and it is not regression. It is your nervous system loosening an identity that can no longer carry you forward.

The solar plexus is also where shame often lives.

Not as a moral failing, but as a bodily contraction, the tightening that happens when a younger part of you learned that being fully yourself was risky. Shame forms around moments of being judged, misunderstood, unseen, or asked to be smaller in order to stay connected.

Thresholds bring this material to the surface not to over-whelm you, but because you cannot step into a truer life while carrying the belief that you must shrink to be loved.

So when shame rises without a clear cause, it is often not about the present moment. It is about an old identity loosening its grip.

This recalibration can feel uncomfortable. You may feel less confident, more sensitive, or uncertain about your place in the world. This is not a loss of strength. It is a release of the kind of strength that requires effort, performance, or self-abandonment to maintain.

As the solar plexus unwinds what never truly belonged to you, there can be a temporary sense of vulnerability. But this clearing creates space for a different kind of strength to form — one rooted in truth rather than survival.

The solar plexus does not work alone.

As thresholds move, different centers respond together. The low belly senses what wants to enter your life. The solar plexus asks what that will require of who you have been. Fear, shame, grief, and longing may all surface at once — not randomly, but in relationship.

This is how identity begins to reorganize.

Not through force or certainty, but through honesty and presence.

The Heart — Where Grief, Softening, and Quiet Knowing Live

If the sacral is where truth first stirs, and the solar plexus is where identity begins to loosen, the heart is where you start to *feel* what the threshold is asking of you.

The heart is not only an emotional center.

It is where the past and the future meet inside your body.

This is where grief often rises, not just grief for what has been lost, but for what is being released. Old identities, familiar ways of coping, versions of yourself that once kept you safe. Even when those versions no longer fit, the heart still needs to acknowledge them.

Because when a threshold opens, you are not only moving toward something new.

You are also leaving something behind.

This is why grief can appear without a clear story. Why sadness and relief may arrive together. Why you might feel unexpectedly tender, or moved by small things, or touched by joy in the middle of heaviness.

This is how the heart speaks when you are changing.

At the same time, tenderness begins to return.

Not as weakness, but as capacity. A sign that something in you is softening enough to be met. The defenses that once held everything together relax just enough to let feeling move again.

And in this softening, a quiet knowing may begin to flicker.

Not as a plan or certainty, but as a subtle sense of direction. A breath that feels like relief. A moment of presence. A gentle pull you can't yet explain. A sense that, even without answers, something is orienting you forward.

These moments don't arrive on command.

They often come after grief has been allowed to move.

The heart is the bridge that makes this possible.

It is where what is emerging becomes felt. Where truth begins to land inside you as lived experience, not just understanding.

This is why the heart can feel raw, open, heavy, hopeful, uncertain, and alive all at once.

Nothing here is fragile.

Something is opening.

The Unseen Companions — How Life Walks With You When You Change

There is a point in every threshold when the heart begins to soften, and in that softening, something else becomes available:

A sense that you are not walking alone.

This awareness doesn't usually arrive as a mystical experience.

It comes through the body, as steadiness, breath, subtle warmth, or the feeling of being gently accompanied from the inside out.

Some people experience this as the presence of the land.

Others feel guided by ancestors or unseen allies.

For some, it is simply a quiet reassurance that life itself is moving with them, not against them.

You do not have to name it for it to be real.

What matters is the **felt sense,** that the same intelligence moving inside your threshold lives in the world around you as well. That the rhythm breathing through wind, water, trees, and stars is the same rhythm reorganizing your inner world.

Support does not always appear as answers.

Often it appears as **companionship.**

A moment when the sky feels closer.

A stone feels like an anchor in your palm.

The ocean steadies your breath.

A candle flickers and you remember you're held.

You speak aloud and it feels like something is listening.

This doesn't mean the path becomes easy.

It means the path is no longer **lonely**.

Thresholds can feel isolating because they change you before language arrives. But the more you soften into what you feel, the more the world meets you in subtle ways through synchronicity, symbolic moments, quiet reassurance, or simply the sense that something kind is walking beside you.

You don't have to believe anything.

You don't have to seek signs.

You don't have to "do" this right.

Just notice what steadies you.

A tree.

A breath.

A prayer.

A stone.

A presence you cannot name.

A feeling of being accompanied rather than abandoned.

This is not fantasy.

It is nervous system truth.

Safety allows connection.

Connection allows trust.

Trust allows the threshold to open.

You do not walk your becoming alone;

You walk it **among companions seen and unseen,
held by a world that recognizes you.**

The Throat — When Truth Pauses Before It Speaks

If the heart is where truth begins to be felt, the throat is where it starts to take shape.

This is why the throat can become tender or reactive during a threshold. It often responds before you consciously know what you are trying to say or whether you are ready to say anything at all.

The throat is closely tied to expression: the ability to speak, to ask, to share what is true. It also carries memory of times you learned to stay quiet, to soften your voice, or to hold things in because it felt safer that way.

So when something new begins to awaken inside you, the throat may tighten.

Not because you are blocked.

But because the truth is still finding its form.

The throat sits at the meeting point between your inner world and the outer one. When these are not yet aligned, the body naturally pauses. You may feel tightness, pressure, or the sense that words stop before they arrive. You may want to speak and feel unable to, or feel the urge to cry without knowing why.

This is not a problem to fix.

Thresholds ask for presence before expression. They ask you to live a truth before you name it.

For many people, this pause brings up fear, especially fear of being misunderstood or judged. Old memories of speaking and being hurt may surface. You may feel unsure how to explain what you are going through, or reluctant to share before you understand it yourself.

Silence here is not avoidance.

It is protection.

The body knows when something is still forming. The throat tightens not to silence you, but to give the truth time to land fully inside you.

There is a natural moment when this changes.

Not suddenly.

Not dramatically.

One day, your voice feels clearer. Not louder, just clearer. The words come without effort because they are no longer trying to outrun your body. They arise from a place that feels lived-in rather than defended.

Until then, the throat simply asks for patience.

Truth does not need to be spoken to be real.

And when it is ready to be spoken, you will not have to force it.

And while the throat learns when to speak and when to rest, something deeper begins to listen, the ground of the body itself.

The Root — Where Ground and Belonging Reorganize

Beneath the low belly lies an even deeper layer of the body, the ground you stand on inside yourself.

The root lives in the pelvis, hips, legs, and the base of the spine. It carries your most fundamental relationship with existence:

Am I safe here?

Do I belong?

Is there ground beneath me?

Is it safe to stay inside myself while life moves?

For many people, this center doesn't react dramatically at first.

It tends to move more slowly, almost cautiously.

It waits to see whether the shifts you are sensing are temporary, imagined, or real.

The sacral may flutter first.

The heart may soften or ache.

The solar plexus may renegotiate identity.

And then, when the change begins to root into reality,
the root quietly recalibrates.

You may feel:

heaviness in the legs

a pull toward rest or being closer to the earth

fatigue that asks you to slow down

or a strange mixture of steadiness and uncertainty.

This is not collapse.

It is **re-grounding.**

The root is the part of you that has held everything together for a very long time. It remembers the environments where you first learned what safety meant not as story, but as atmosphere. So when change arrives, the root naturally asks:

"Can this new truth exist — while I remain here, steady, inside myself?"

Sometimes the root tightens while it evaluates.

Sometimes it softens because something truer has finally arrived.

Sometimes it asks you to move more slowly than your mind prefers.

None of this is resistance.

It is **care.**

The root does not chase change.

It waits until the rest of you is ready

and then it reorganizes the ground beneath your life.

When this happens, there is often a subtle shift:

- your breath deepens
- your step feels heavier in a good way
- your body feels more *inside itself*
- urgency fades
- stillness becomes possible

Not because the threshold has ended
but because **your ground now includes the truth that once felt threatening.**

And beneath all of this, the nervous system is quietly tracking every shift. It is the part of you that decides the pace not from judgment, but from care.

The Nervous System — The Gatekeeper of Every Threshold

If the soul initiates a threshold, the nervous system sets the pace.

This is the part most people are never taught to consider. It's why so much spiritual language can feel frustrating or shaming, as if change should happen simply because we understand it, intend it, or want it badly enough.

But thresholds do not move at the speed of thought.

They move at the speed of safety.

You cannot pass through a threshold faster than your nervous system can reorganize. This is not a flaw or a limitation. It is the body's intelligence at work.

Every threshold involves something dissolving, something emerging, and something reorienting. The nervous system is the part of you that quietly assesses whether this movement can happen without overwhelming what still needs care.

This is why thresholds feel so physical, even when they are

emotional or spiritual. The body is learning whether it is safe to let go of what it has known, and whether it can hold what is coming next.

As this happens, the nervous system moves in waves. Tightening and releasing. Fear and relief. Fatigue followed by presence. Clarity appearing and disappearing again. This is not instability. It is integration.

Thresholds do not unfold in straight lines. They spiral. What you feel one day may not match the next, and that does not mean you are moving backward. It means your system is working in layers, the same way you lived your life in layers.

Even changes you deeply desire can activate resistance here. The nervous system is wired for familiarity before fulfillment. It remembers what once kept you safe, even if it no longer fits. This is why longing and fear often rise together during thresholds.

The real question is not how quickly you can change.

It is whether you can stay with yourself while change is happening.

When you can remain present in the contraction without forcing clarity, without abandoning yourself, something important shifts. The nervous system begins to recognize that it is safe enough to continue.

This recognition does not arrive as certainty.

It arrives as steadiness.

A little more breath.

A little more space.

A sense of being inside yourself rather than bracing against life.

This is not the end of the threshold.

It is the point where the threshold becomes livable.

Walking the Threshold from the Inside

At some point in every threshold, the question stops being *What is happening to me?*

And becomes *Can I stay with myself while this happens?*

By now, you may recognize that change does not move through you all at once. It travels in layers, through sensation, identity, emotion, expression, and regulation. It rises, recedes, and rises again. Some days you may feel open and clear. Other days are heavy, uncertain, or tender. This is not a sign that something has gone wrong. It is the body doing its work.

Thresholds are not crossed by understanding them.

They are crossed by walking them from the inside.

You may notice sensation first, a tightening in the belly, a pressure in the chest, a fatigue you can't explain, a quiet restlessness that won't leave you alone. These sensations are not problems to solve. They are information. They tell you where something is reorganizing, where an old story is loosening, where a new truth is beginning to take shape.

The body does not speak in conclusions.

It speaks in signals.

Listening inside a threshold does not require special skills or spiritual insight. It requires slowness. It asks you to turn toward what you feel without rushing to interpret it. To name sensation without attaching a story. To pause when the body asks for rest. To stop when you feel done.

Often, what the body needs is simple — a slower breath, a hand placed gently where sensation is strongest, a moment of quiet, a sip of water, a few minutes of grounding. These small acts of attention tell the nervous system something essential: *I am here. I am listening. I am not abandoning myself.*

This is how thresholds move.

Not through intensity, effort, or force but through companionship.

As you stay with yourself, you may notice that what once felt overwhelming begins to soften. Tears may come and go. Emotion may rise and pass without explanation. Clarity may flicker, disappear, and return again later in a different form. This does not mean you are going backward. It means your system is integrating change at a pace it can sustain.

At times, it may feel as though you are unraveling, old fears surfacing, younger parts appearing, familiar coping patterns losing their grip. This is not collapse; it is release. The body letting go of what it no longer needs to carry forward.

And then, often quietly, something shifts.

You may find yourself breathing more deeply without trying. Feeling more present in your body. Less compelled to figure everything out. More able to sit with uncertainty without panic. You may begin making different choices not because you decided to change, but because the old ones no longer feel true.

This is reorganization — the quiet process by which the body integrates what the mind has not yet caught up to. Not breakdown.

This is what happens when you stop fighting the threshold.

Emergence does not arrive as a dramatic breakthrough. It arrives as a subtle remembering. A sense of steadiness returning. A quiet trust in yourself that does not require proof. A feeling of being more *inside* your life than braced against it.

You may even recognize the feeling and think, *I feel like myself again.*

Only softer.

Clearer.

More honest.

This is not the end of change. Thresholds will continue to

appear throughout your life. But when you learn how to walk them from the inside, how to listen, how to pause, how to stay, they no longer feel like something is happening *to* you.

They become something moving *through* you.

And you begin to recognize the truth beneath every threshold:

You were never lost.

You were being reorganized around who you truly are.

This is the body's wisdom.

This is the quiet intelligence of change.

And this is how you learn to walk forward, not with certainty, but with presence.

3

HOW WE GET LOST — AND WHY THRESHOLDS CALL US BACK

The Quiet Ways We Drift From Ourselves

People often believe they lost themselves in one moment, a crisis, a heartbreak, a trauma, a wrong turn, a choice that pulled them off course.

But the truth is usually gentler.

We rarely lose ourselves all at once.

We drift, slowly, quietly, unconsciously, until one day we realize we can't feel our own center.

And the reason isn't failure.

It's protection.

At every age, your system chose what felt safest. And what felt safest gradually became who you thought you were.

Not your soul.

Not your deepest truth.

But the version of you that helped you survive your world.

There are quiet ways this drifting happens.

Sometimes we dim parts of ourselves to stay connected.

As children, connection is survival. We will trade authenticity for belonging without knowing we're doing it.

We learn which emotions are welcome.

Which needs get met.

Which truths are safe to speak.

Which parts of us are "too much."

Which behaviors bring approval.

Which versions of us keep the peace.

Piece by piece, we shape ourselves around what keeps love close.

Sometimes we build identities around what hurts the least.

Children don't say, "They didn't know how to meet my needs."

Children say, "It must be me."

So we form conclusions that aren't conscious thoughts —
they are emotional agreements with life:

I must not need.

I must not feel.

I must not express.

I must be easier.

I must be smaller.

I must be strong.

I must be invisible.

I must earn love.

Those conclusions become identities.

Identities become patterns.

Patterns become the invisible architecture of our life.

Sometimes we learn to navigate through doubt.

Most people assume they doubt themselves because they are
insecure. But often doubt is strategy, the nervous system
trying to soften pain before it arrives.

*If I question myself first, it won't hurt as much when someone else
questions me.*

If I doubt my desires, I won't risk disappointment.

If I question my truth, I won't risk conflict.

Doubt isn't a flaw.

It's self-protection that became familiar enough to feel like home.

Sometimes we lose contact with the body because the body tells too much truth.

The body knows what is needed.

What is misaligned.

What is ending.

What is beginning.

But if listening to the body would have created conflict, loss, or danger earlier in life, we learned to disconnect.

I'll feel later.

I don't have time for this.

This is too much.

I can't break down.

We stop listening long before the body stops speaking.

And sometimes we adapt so well that we forget we're

adapting.

This is one of the most painful realities:

The self you had to become to survive can be so convincing that you forget it isn't who you truly are.

You become the strong one.

The healer.

The caretaker.

The high achiever.

The one who holds everything.

The one who doesn't need.

The one who stays quiet.

The one who makes it easier for everyone else.

These roles become armor. They protect you.

And they also separate you from the you underneath.

This is how we get lost.

Not dramatically.

Not instantly.

Quietly, over time, until one day you realize the life you're living is too small for who you actually are.

And that is exactly why thresholds arise.

Thresholds are not punishments.

They are not chaos.

They are not proof that something is wrong.

They are invitations:

You are growing out of the person you had to become.

Are you willing to meet the person you actually are?

The Moment You Realize You're No Longer Who You Once Were

There comes a moment — sometimes sudden, sometimes subtle — when you feel something inside you shift.

It rarely comes with clarity.

It rarely arrives with a plan.

It often comes as restlessness.

A sense of being out of place.

Unexpected tears.

Old patterns feeling too tight.

Familiar roles suddenly feeling heavy.

A quiet ache.

A subtle pressure in the belly or the chest.

The sense that something is "off," even when nothing looks different.

This moment is disorienting because the outer world hasn't changed but the inner world already has.

The old identity begins dissolving faster than the new one can form.

You enter the in-between, the place where:

- the identity that once protected you feels too small
- the life built around that identity starts to feel outgrown
- the strategies that once kept you safe no longer fit
- what you used to tolerate becomes intolerable
- the mask you wore starts slipping
- the truth inside you becomes harder to ignore

And because most people were never taught what this is, they interpret it as failure:

I'm confused.

I'm overwhelmed.

I'm going backward.

I don't know who I am.

Something must be wrong.

But this moment is not regression.

It's revelation.

Your system is showing you:

You are no longer this version of yourself.

You can't force yourself back into who you used to be.

This identity cannot carry you forward.

You are becoming someone else — even if you can't see her yet.

This moment can feel like fear because it requires unfamiliar capacity.

In threshold work, fear rarely means danger.

Often it means unfamiliarity.

Fear is the nervous system saying:

I don't know how to be this new yet.

I've never lived from this truth before.

I don't know if it's safe to expand.

And this moment can feel like grief because you're losing something, even if you didn't love it.

The body grieves familiarity.

Not because you want the old life back, but because it knew how to navigate it.

Confusion does not mean you don't know.

It often means the knowing you lived by is dissolving.

This is where thresholds do their deepest work.

You haven't lost yourself.

You've lost the layer that was hiding you.

You are not falling apart.

You are falling inward.

This is the beginning of the path home.

When the Mind Panics and the Soul Moves First

There is a moment in every threshold when something inside you begins to move — quietly, subtly, unmistakably.

You feel a pull you can't explain.

A truth you can't yet name.

A sense that life is shifting, even though nothing looks different.

This is a soul shift.

And almost always, as soon as it begins, the mind panics.

Not because anything is wrong but because the soul is moving in a direction the mind cannot yet understand.

The mind is built on memory: what has happened, what has been survived, what has kept you safe.

The soul moves from knowing: what is true, what is emerging, what is calling you forward.

When the soul begins to lead, the mind loses its orientation. It cannot rely on the old map, so it reacts as if you're in danger:

What if I'm wrong?

I can't trust this feeling.

Everything feels uncertain.

I don't know what I'm doing.

But these thoughts are not signs you're off track.

They are signs the soul is already one step ahead.

A soul shift does not begin with clarity.

It begins with disruption.

Your old desires no longer fit.

Your old patterns feel too tight.

Your old way of being stops working.

And the mind calls that "panic," when the soul is simply calling it *movement.*

You don't need to silence the mind.

You need to guide it.

I hear you.

I know you're afraid.

But nothing is wrong.

Something new is becoming possible.

When the adult self speaks with steadiness, the mind settles, and the soul's movement becomes clearer.

You may not yet know where you're going.

You may not know why the change is happening.

You may not feel ready.

You don't need to.

A soul shift does not require understanding, only willingness.

Resistance: The Protective Intelligence at the Doorway

If becoming your truest self were simple, you would have already become her.

But we don't, not because we're weak, not because we're broken, not because we're behind.

We resist because transformation asks us to touch the very places we learned to avoid.

Resistance isn't the enemy.

Resistance is information.

It often rises because:

- we fear losing the roles that once kept us safe
- we fear the responsibility of living from truth
- the nervous system equates unfamiliarity with danger
- we fear the grief of letting go
- we fear being seen
- we fear the dissolution of the story that gave our life structure

Even painful stories can feel like home.

So resistance appears.

Not to stop your growth but to slow it enough that your tenderness can stay intact.

This is important:

Resistance is not the end of transformation.

It is the beginning.

It is the protective self saying:

I'm afraid.

I need time.

I need gentleness.

I need reassurance.

I need you here with me.

When you meet resistance with presence instead of force, it transforms.

Not because you conquered it but because you stopped abandoning yourself inside it.

Is This a Threshold or Fear? A Simple Discernment

Not every discomfort is a threshold.

Not every impulse is truth.

Not every emotional surge is transformation.

Some movements are fear.

Some are old loops.

Some are fantasies of escape.

Some are protective parts trying to pull you back into the familiar.

A true threshold has a different signature.

A threshold is usually **quiet and persistent**, not dramatic and urgent.

It doesn't scream. It waits.

Here's one of the simplest ways to tell:

Fear comes with a story.

What if I fail? What if I'm wrong? What if I lose?

A threshold comes with a sensation.

A pull. A pressure. A tightening. A shift in breath.

Something you can't explain, but you can feel.

Fear spikes and flares.

A threshold settles in and stays.

Fear pushes you to hurry.

A threshold asks you to slow down.

Fear contracts you into defense.

A threshold often makes you tender, even when you're afraid.

Fear makes you want to escape.

A threshold makes you want to pause and listen.

Here is the clearest signature:

A threshold doesn't demand a leap.

It asks for presence.

And when the time is right, something inside you releases and says:

Now.

That "now" is unmistakable.

It doesn't feel like pressure.

It feels like alignment.

The Invitation: The Path Home Begins Here

This is why thresholds exist.

Not to break you.

Not to punish you.

Not to destabilize you for no reason.

Thresholds arise when the life you are living can no longer
hold the truth you are becoming.

They call you back:

to your body,

to your breath,

to your inner honesty,

to the parts of you that learned to survive without being
held.

A threshold is life saying:

Come back.

Come closer.

Come home.

And the next question becomes not, *How do I fix this?*

But:

How do I stay with myself while I change?

That is where we go next.

4

HOW TO STAY WITH YOURSELF WHEN EVERYTHING IS CHANGING

There is a moment in every inner transition where you realize the change is not something happening *to* you, it is something happening *within* you.

It shifts your breath.

It shifts your perception.

It shifts the way you move through the world.

You feel the tremor of becoming.

And with that awareness comes a quiet truth:

The most important thing you can do in any threshold is stay with yourself.

Not stay ahead of yourself.

Not stay in what you *think* you should be feeling.

Not stay in the version of you that existed before.

Stay with the self who is here now, in this exact moment of becoming.

We weren't taught how to do that.

We were taught the opposite.

Many of us learned to leave ourselves to stay safe.

To avoid conflict.

To keep the peace.

To be acceptable.

To survive.

To belong.

So staying with yourself is not just a spiritual practice.

It is an act of reclamation.

It is how you become whole again.

This chapter is about learning to stay with honesty, tenderness, and presence, especially when it feels hardest.

Why Staying With Yourself Feels Hard and Why It's the Medicine a Threshold Requires

Staying with yourself sounds simple.

But it goes against what most of us learned:

Ignore your body.

Override your needs.

Explain your emotions.

Silence your intuition.

Keep going.

So when a threshold arrives, one of the first truths you may feel is:

"I don't know how to stay with what's happening inside me."

Here's why it feels hard and why it matters.

Presence activates what you once had to avoid.

Presence reveals what hurts, what is tender, what is unfinished, what is dissolving, what is rising.

It brings truth into the light.

So the protective parts resist — not because you're broken, but because presence asks you to meet what's real.

And what's real invites change.

Your system learned to think instead of feel.

Thinking became a substitute for emotional safety.

So the moment sensation rises, your system may reach for: analysis, planning, controlling, distracting, performing, numbing.

Not because you're doing something wrong.

Because feeling requires vulnerability and vulnerability used to feel unsafe.

Thresholds awaken younger selves.

Not as regression, as *reorganization.*

A younger part rises because it carried the pattern you are outgrowing.

Staying means you become the adult your younger part needed.

That's why it's tender.

That's why it's holy.

Staying interrupts old safety strategies.

- People-pleasing.
- Disappearing.
- Fixing.

- Over-performing.
- Staying silent.
- Over-explaining.
- Controlling.

These weren't failures.

They were survival.

But thresholds are where survival strategies get renegotiated.

And staying is how you do it.

The deeper truth.

Thresholds don't require perfection.

They require **return**.

Return to breath.

Return to body.

Return to honesty.

Return to the moment you're actually in.

Staying with yourself is what keeps a threshold from becoming a crisis and allows it to become a passage.

* * *

Micro-practice: The 10-second return

Hand to belly.

One slow exhale.

Whisper: *"I'm here."*

That's enough to begin.

* * *

The Three Selves You Meet in Every Threshold

Younger Self, Adult Self, Soul Self

Every threshold brings three layers of you into the same room:

- **The younger self** who learned how to survive
- **The adult self** who can stay, regulate, and choose
- **The soul self** who is guiding the deeper unfolding knows truth before you can name it

The mind is not separate from these, it simply speaks differently depending on which self it is serving. Confusion happens when one layer runs the whole moment.

The Younger Self

This is the emotional imprint, the part that adapted early, held the fear, and built the strategy.

You may notice: vulnerability that feels "too young," emotional waves, the impulse to hide, cling, freeze, disappear.

These are not regressions.

They are memories asking for company.

The Adult Self

Not the "strong" mask.

Not the part that performs being okay.

The adult self is your capacity to stay.

It says:

"I'm here."

"We can slow down."

"You're safe with me."

"We don't have to solve this."

This is the self that rewires the nervous system.

The Soul Self

The compass. The deeper truth. The initiator.

It speaks through: felt sense, resonance, timing, intuition, dream-language, synchronicity, the quiet certainty of *this is true*.

It does not panic.

It does not rush.

It moves with precision.

How they work together

- The younger self **feels**
- The adult self **stays**
- The soul self **leads**

* * *

Practice - Learning Which Part of You is Speaking

Step 1 — Ask one simple question (about 5 seconds).

Place a hand on your chest or belly and ask:

"Which part of me is closest right now?"

Don't analyze. Just notice.

Step 2 — Choose the closest match (without over-thinking).

Younger Self signs.

You may feel:

- small or exposed
- urgent or needy
- panicky or frozen
- ashamed
- overwhelmed
- like *"I can't."*

This part speaks in **feeling and protection.**

Adult Self signs.

You may notice:

- grounded awareness
- a steadier inner tone
- the ability to stay present
- a willingness to take one small step
- language like *"This is hard — and I can be with it."*

This part speaks in **capacity and kindness.**

Soul Self signs.

This arrives as:

- quiet
- steady
- simple
- a felt *yes or no*
- a subtle orientation

- no rush

This part doesn't argue.

It feels like **space.**

If the Mind is Racing.

Looping thoughts, problem-solving, rehearsing, catastrophizing, or demanding certainty usually mean:

the Younger Self is afraid

and the Mind is trying to protect you.

Nothing is wrong.

We simply bring the Adult Self forward again.

Step 3 — Offer the response that matches (30–60 seconds).

If the Younger Self is closest → "Contain + Contact"

Place one hand on your belly, one on your heart.

Exhale slowly, as if gently fogging a mirror.

Then say softly (out loud if possible):

"I'm here with you.

You don't have to do this alone.

We're not fixing anything right now."

Then ask only: ***"What do you need in the next 10 minutes?"***

Keep the answer small, like:

- water
- rest
- to step outside
- a blanket
- to text someone safe

This part needs companionship — not correction.

If the Adult Self is present → "Stay + Support"

Let the steadiness lead.

You might say:

"I can stay with this.

One thing at a time is enough."

Then choose **one grounded action**, such as:

- sit back in your chair
- feel your feet on the floor
- take one gentle breath
- do the next right-sized task

This builds trust in your own presence.

If the Soul Self is speaking → "One Quiet Truth"

Slow your movements by about 10%.

Soften your jaw.

Let the breath deepen naturally.

Ask:

"What is one true sentence right now?"

It might be:

"I'm not ready yet."

"This matters."

"I need space."

"Something in me is changing."

Stop there.

No plan. No pressure.

Truth does not rush.

If the Mind is Overactive → "Name + Narrow"

This is not a problem — just a signal.

Gently look around and name **three neutral things:**

"chair... window... cup..."

Then name **one sensation:**

"tight chest." "heavy belly." "warm face."

Say:

"My mind is trying to help.

I'm returning to the body now."

Take **three ordinary breaths**, paying soft attention to the exhale.

That's all.

Not analysis.

Not self-improvement.

Just **recognition + companionship.**

This is discernment made livable.

* * *

How to Recognize When You've Left Yourself and How to Gently Come Back

Most people don't struggle because they leave themselves.

They struggle because they don't notice when it happens.

You've left yourself when:

- your mind speeds up into loops

- you override sensation
- you go into performance (*"I'm fine"*)
- you try to fix, control, or force clarity
- you collapse into hopelessness or numbness
- you stop naming small truths
- you reject your tenderness

The return is simple.

Not easy, simple.

A gentle way back

1. **Name what's true**: *"My chest is tight."*
2. **Touch one place**: hand to chest/belly/throat
3. **One long exhale**
4. **One sentence**: *"I'm here. I'm not leaving."*

Your return is always more important than how far you drifted.

Every return strengthens your adult self.

Every return teaches your system: *"We are safe to keep going."*

Building an Inner Ground You Can Return To — No Matter What Changes Around You

In thresholds, the inner world can feel unfamiliar.

Not broken.

Just unfamiliar.

So you need something sturdier than confidence.

Something more reliable than clarity.

Inner ground is made of contact.

Contact with breath.

Contact with body.

Contact with truth.

Contact with the younger self.

Contact with the moment.

Inner ground isn't built through dramatic practices.

It's built through small acts of staying:

A sigh you allow.

A jaw you soften.

A truth you admit.

A boundary you honor.

A moment you stop pushing.

Inner ground is not a technique.

It is a relationship cultivated through return, return, return.

How to Stay With Yourself Through Fear, Doubt, and Disorientation

Thresholds don't open when life is convenient.

They open in the middle of your real life.

So fear, doubt, and disorientation are not signs you're wrong.

They're signs you're touching unfamiliar capacity.

Fear.

Fear is protective — not prophetic.

Stay with it like this:

"I feel fear, and I'm here."

"I feel trembling, and I'm not leaving."

Doubt.

Doubt is the mind losing prediction.

Try:

"Something new is forming that I can't understand yet."

"I don't need to know. I need to stay."

Disorientation.

Disorientation is re-mapping.

Anchor into one thing: your feet, your exhale, the weight of your body, one object in the room.

The body doesn't need the full map.

It needs this moment.

* * *

Practice: The Single Anchor (3 breaths)

Choose **one** anchor below and stay with it for **three exhales**:

1. **Feet Anchor**
2. Press your feet into the floor like you're leaving a footprint.
3. Notice: pressure in heels / balls of feet.
4. **Hand Anchor**
5. Place a palm on your chest or belly.
6. Notice: warmth, weight, contact.
7. **Exhale Anchor**
8. Breathe out slowly through the mouth (like cooling soup).
9. Notice: the end of the exhale.
10. **Sight Anchor**
11. Pick one object and look at its edges.
12. Notice: shape, color, texture.

If you drift, you don't start over, you simply come back to the same anchor.

* * *

How Staying With Yourself Changes Everything

When you stop abandoning yourself, life begins reorganizing around that truth.

- Your nervous system learns safety from the inside
- Discomfort becomes communication, not danger
- Your inner authority grows quieter and stronger
- Relationships reorganize toward honesty and reciprocity
- Your path becomes clearer through felt sense, not force
- You become someone who can walk through change without losing yourself

This is the quiet miracle:

You stop fearing thresholds because you no longer fear abandonment, not from others, but from yourself.

Staying becomes the path.

Staying becomes the doorway.

Staying becomes home.

And from that home, you're ready for what comes next: **the in-between — when you're no longer who you were, and not yet who you're becoming.**

5

THE IN-BETWEEN: WHEN YOU ARE NO LONGER WHO YOU WERE

There is a place in every transformation where the old self has loosened but the new self has not yet arrived. You can feel the dissolution — the unraveling of patterns, the shifting of identity, the release of old protections. But you cannot yet feel what comes next. The clarity hasn't arrived. The direction hasn't formed. The version of you that is becoming hasn't grown solid enough to stand in yet.

This place is not a mistake.

It is a passage.

It is called the in-between, and it is one of the most sacred and most misunderstood phases of human becoming. Not comfortable, but holy. Not stable, but precise. Not obvious, but deeply intelligent.

Why It Feels So Unsettling

The in-between is one of the most honest places a human being can stand. It is where the old story no longer fits, but the new one hasn't found its language yet. Where your inner world has already shifted, but your outer life hasn't caught up. Where you've outgrown who you were, but haven't yet stepped into who you're becoming.

Nothing is wrong. And yet nothing feels stable.

The unsettling quality of this phase comes from the fact that you are in direct contact with truth — a truth your mind doesn't have a category for yet. The mind needs continuity. It needs a storyline, a familiar reference point, a sense of what comes next. When the old identity dissolves, those reference points disappear, and the mind cannot orient the way it used to. This is not regression. It is the soul dismantling scaffolding that once protected you, but that you no longer need.

Alongside this, your nervous system loses its familiar cues. Even old patterns you didn't want still felt known. When they drop, the system briefly loses its footing — not because you are unstable, but because new wiring hasn't finished forming yet. This is a sign of progress, even when it feels like the opposite.

Something else happens here too. Your inner pace slows — naturally, not through effort. Thoughts quiet. Desires soften. Direction blurs. Impulses settle. This slowing isn't stagnation. It is gestation. The soul doesn't reorganize you at the speed of fear or urgency. It reorganizes you at the speed of truth. The in-between is the womb of becoming.

You may also find yourself more sensitive than usual — more attuned to mismatches, longing, grief, and tenderness. This is not fragility. It is proximity. When you are close to your soul, you feel everything the soul wants you to notice. This heightened sensitivity is actually alignment calling your name.

And perhaps most disorienting of all: you can no longer go back, but you cannot yet move forward. The old door is closed. The new one hasn't opened. You are standing in the hallway between lifetimes of yourself. Most people try to escape this space through urgency, distraction, or forcing clarity. But the in-between is not a space to escape. It is a space to receive. The very tension you feel is the pressure that forms the next version of you. It is not a trap. It is a crucible.

The Three Signs You've Entered This Passage

Most people cross into the in-between without recognizing where they are. They assume something is wrong. They assume they have lost direction or fallen behind. But the in-between is not a detour. It is the natural middle space between who you were and who you are becoming. Here is how you know you have entered it.

The first sign is that the old way no longer works, but the new way hasn't arrived yet. Your old patterns, identities, and strategies stop functioning the way they used to. You can't force motivation the way you once did. You can't perform old roles without feeling drained. You can't pretend something fits when it's quietly dissolving. Your system is refusing to return to a version of you that no longer exists. This is not collapse. It is liberation.

The second sign is that your inner world feels mismatched with your outer world. You have shifted internally, but your relationships, work, environment, and daily life haven't yet rearranged to reflect it. There is a subtle friction — an inner restlessness, a quiet sense of holding something you haven't yet named or stepped into. Your soul is ahead of your life. This is not misalignment. It is alignment catching up.

The third sign is that you can feel something forming, but you cannot describe it yet. There is a presence approaching — a new path, a new way of being — and you can sense it like a shape behind a thin veil. You can't name it. You can't plan around it. You can't make it arrive faster. But you feel it: a subtle excitement, a quiet fear, an anticipation mixed with grief, a sense that something is dissolving to make space for something else. This is not confusion. This is emergence. The soul works this way — first sensation, then language, then form.

These three signs are not symptoms of being lost. They are the fingerprints of becoming.

* * *

Practice: The 'This Is Different' Check (90 seconds)

This is for the moment you think: I'm failing. I'm behind. I'm going backwards.

Place one hand on your chest or belly. Look around the room and name five ordinary things you can see — without rushing. Then quietly ask: Is this now, or is this then?

Without forcing an answer, notice what happens in your body. Does your breath drop even a little? Does your jaw unclench? Does your belly soften? Even a small shift is information. It means your system has more capacity than it did before — which means you are not back at the beginning. You are meeting something familiar from a new place.

* * *

How to Navigate Life When Nothing Feels Solid

When you enter the in-between, certainty dissolves. Not because you are making a mistake, but because your soul refuses to let you live by an old map. You don't know what you want yet. You don't know what you're becoming. And the mind, which is built on prediction and pattern, finds this deeply uncomfortable.

What stabilizes you here is not clarity — it is contact. Contact with your breath. Contact with your body. Contact with the small truths available to you right now.

The first thing the in-between asks of you is simplicity. When direction disappears, the instinct is to fill the void with decisions, plans, and urgency. But this phase requires the opposite. Fewer obligations. Fewer internal demands. Less multitasking. Gentle mornings. Early nights. Simple meals. Your life shrinks so your soul can expand.

Rather than goals — which require a clarity you don't yet have — anchor yourself in rhythm. Drink water when you wake. Sit with your breath for a moment. Feel your feet on the ground. Step outside for a minute of air. These small touch points of connection with yourself create a steadiness that no amount of planning can provide.

Rhythm stabilizes what clarity cannot.

When you do need to make decisions, notice whether they arise from urgency or from softness. Urgency is the nervous system saying: I'm scared. Softness is the soul saying: I'm listening. If a decision feels tight, pressured, or born from anxiety, pause. If it feels quiet, warm, or like a subtle yes in the body, trust it. During the in-between, the mind pushes and the soul nudges. Follow the nudge.

Your body remains your compass when your mind cannot guide you. Ask it: *What does my chest feel like right now? My belly? My throat?* The body does not lie. It communicates in real time, and it knows what is true even when the mind feels empty.

And when you notice others moving faster, seeming clearer, appearing more certain — let them. You are resting in the soil before a new season. Your timeline is not late. It is precise.

Use the smallest truths as guideposts. In the in-between, your big truths may be hidden, but your small truths are available: *I'm tired. I don't know. I need rest. This feels too much. I feel drawn to this. I want something simpler.* Small truths create pathways to larger ones. They are how the soul guides you when the next version of yourself is still forming.

And trust that what feels like nothing happening is actually everything happening. Beneath the stillness, your soul is building a new orientation. Your nervous system is rewiring safety. Your identity is rearranging. Your old templates are dissolving. The stillness is not emptiness. It is construction.

* * *

Practice: Rhythm Before Answers (3 minutes)

This is for days when you don't know what you want, and your mind keeps demanding a plan.

Choose one small act of grounding rhythm and do it once today, slowly: Drink a full glass of water while standing still, feeling your feet. Or step outside for one minute, letting air touch your face. Or wash your hands and feel the water as if it is bringing you back. Or put a hand on your heart and take one long exhale before you speak.

The point is not the habit. The point is the message your system receives: I am here. I am with myself. I do not have to force clarity.

* * *

How to Stay Oriented When You Can't Feel the Future Yet

One of the hardest parts of the in-between is the absence of orientation. The future feels out of reach. The old map doesn't apply. Your intuition feels muffled and your direction foggy. This is not a sign that you are doing something wrong. It is a sign that your identity is being rewritten faster than your mind can comprehend.

You do not need clarity right now. You need a different

kind of orientation — not based on certainty or goals, but on presence. On truth. On moment-to-moment listening.

The mind, when the future is unclear, tries to leap ahead: *What am I supposed to do? How do I prepare? What if I choose wrong?* But during the in-between, the only reliable place to orient is the present moment. Not the future. Not the mind's projections. Ask instead: *What is true right now? What is needed right now? What can I feel in my body right now?* Orientation emerges through presence long before it emerges through clarity.

Rather than asking what you are supposed to do next, try asking what is quietly calling you right now. Not the big calling. Not the life-purpose calling. The small, immediate calling: rest, a walk, writing, a conversation, silence, sunlight, tears. When you honor the small callings, the larger ones reveal themselves.

Don't mistake lack of clarity for lack of progress. Clarity is a late stage of transformation. It often arrives at the end of a release, at the end of a deep rest cycle, at the end of internal rearrangement — not at the beginning. The absence of clarity is not the absence of movement. It is the space that clarity needs in order to land.

And consider this: you don't have to hunt for your path. Your future is not something you choose — it is something you recognize when it steps into your field. Direction arrives through synchronicities, unexpected opportunities, subtle pulls, a sudden internal shift, a surprising yes, a soft no, a door opening without effort. When you stop grasping for clarity, clarity finds you.

When you cannot feel the future, feel yourself. Your breath. Your body. Your honesty. Your presence. Your truth. If you can feel yourself, you are oriented. The future will find you from there.

* * *

Practice: Orientation Through Contact (2–4 minutes)

This is for the fog days, when you can't feel intuition, desire, or direction.

Put both feet on the floor. Press them down just enough to feel your legs engage. Rub your palms together for ten seconds and place them on your thighs, belly, or heart. Choose one anchor — the weight of your body in the chair, the feeling of your feet on the ground, the rise and fall of your breath — and stay with it for three breaths. When your mind leaps ahead, come back to the single sensation. You don't need a map. You need contact.

* * *

How to Trust the Process When It Feels Like You're Going Backwards

There is a moment in every transformation when it feels like everything is unraveling.

Old emotions return. Old patterns resurface. Old fears come forward. Old doubts whisper through the mind. It can feel like losing progress, like slipping back, like you've returned to where you started.

But this experience is not regression. It is refinement. Integration. Depth.

When old material rises, it surfaces not because you've gone backward, but because you are more resourced than before — safer, stronger, more conscious — and your system is finally ready to release what it could not release before. These emotions are completing what was never finished. Healing moves in spirals, not straight lines. You are meeting the same material, but from a higher rung of the spiral.

The mind will tell you otherwise. It likes predictable patterns, and when you reach a new layer of becoming, when the old way no longer works, it panics: This is bad. This is wrong. This doesn't feel like me. But unfamiliar doesn't mean wrong. It means new. You are moving forward into a place that has no familiar reference yet.

When a pattern resurfaces, don't ask whether it's the same as before. Ask whether it feels as overwhelming as before. Do you notice it sooner? Does it pass more quickly? Do you recover more easily? Are you observing it instead of drowning in it? Are you telling the truth faster? These shifts are signs of progress, even when the content feels familiar. The pattern is dissolving from the inside out.

The deeper the threshold, the more old material rises. This doesn't mean something has gone wrong. It means the shift is penetrating the structures that once defined your identity. Old material comes up because it cannot come with you. Dissolution is not collapse. It is preparation.

When fear returns, anchor into what is true rather than into

the story the mind tells. The mind narrates through fear:
You're failing. You're back at the beginning. You're stuck.

The soul narrates through sensation: *I'm meeting another layer. My system is ready for this. This sensation has been here for years — now I can finally feel it. This is not regression. This is release.*

Every time an old pattern rises, you have two paths: leave yourself, or stay with yourself.

Staying is what transforms the pattern into wisdom. Staying is what integrates the younger self. Staying is what breaks the loop. You don't need to do it perfectly. Just honestly. Staying is the way through.

* * *

Practice: Spiral, Not Setback (2 minutes)

This is for the moment when an old fear returns and shame tries to narrate it.

Put a hand on the place in your body where you feel it today — belly, throat, chest, back. Don't analyze. Just locate. Then say one sentence, slowly: This is the old thing, in a new body. Take one long exhale. Then ask: What is different this time? Not what is the same. What is different? You noticed sooner. You're telling the truth faster. You're not collapsing in the same way. Even one difference is proof of integration. This isn't a return to the beginning. It is the spiral tightening toward freedom.

6

WHAT IS HAPPENING
BENEATH THE SURFACE

When nothing in your outer life seems to be moving, your inner life is working the hardest.

The mind sees stillness. The ego sees confusion. The nervous system feels unsettled. But something deeper — the quiet intelligence of your being — is moving with extraordinary precision. The in-between is not a passive space. It is an active reorganization. And understanding what is actually happening beneath the surface can transform the way you relate to this phase, from something you endure to something you trust.

Dissolving the Identity That Was Built for Survival

Before a new identity can form, the soul begins dissolving the one that was shaped by fear, approval, conditioning, and old loyalty. The self you learned to be — cautious, performing, adapting, holding — begins to loosen. This dissolution feels disorienting from the inside: *I don't know who I am anymore. I don't want what I used to want. I can't pretend to be that person. I don't fit into that life.*

But this is not loss. It is the shedding of what you were required to be. And underneath it, something truer is waiting.

Clearing What Was Never Yours

The in-between is also a cleansing cycle. Your system releases old fears, inherited beliefs, internalized voices, family patterns, societal expectations, and energetic residues that accumulated over a lifetime. This clearing can feel like fatigue, fog, unexplainable emotions, waves of grief followed by surprising waves of relief. Random memories may surface. Old sensations return. You may feel empty in a way that isn't painful — just spacious.

This is your system making space for a self you have not yet met.

Recalibrating Your Nervous System

Old survival responses cannot support a new version of you. So during the in-between, the nervous system quietly recalibrates. The patterns that once kept you alert — bracing, scanning, fawning, fleeing — begin to soften. This recalibration feels, from the inside, like tiredness. Less motivation. An unusual calm. Needing more rest and less stimulation. You may wonder if something is wrong.

Nothing is wrong. Your system is learning to live in a place of greater truth. What feels like regression is actually an upgrade.

Reorienting Your Inner Compass

Before this threshold, your inner compass was likely set by what you feared — what you wanted to avoid, what would keep the peace, what was expected of you. In the in-between, the soul begins resetting this compass. You start to orient through sensation, felt truth, curiosity, ease, and resonance rather than through avoidance and performance.

This shift feels like a quiet refusal: *I don't want to live like that anymore. I don't know what's next, but it isn't this. I need something truer.* This is not confusion. It is reorientation.

Calling Back the Parts of You That Were Exiled

Thresholds pull older selves forward. The seven-year-old who learned to hide. The adolescent who learned to perform. The young adult who learned to endure. These parts rise not to create chaos, but to come home. They appear as unexpected emotions, sudden insecurities, old memories, younger voices in your mind, or childhood sensations in the body. They are asking to be recognized — not corrected.

You cannot fully step into the next version of yourself while split from the earlier versions of yourself. The wholeness that is forming requires all of you.

Strengthening the Self Who Will Carry You Forward

Quietly, even in the fog, the adult self is becoming more capable. The part of you that can hold truth, stay steady, listen inward, set limits, and navigate discomfort is being strengthened — not through effort, but through the slow practice of staying with yourself across the weeks and months of this passage. You may notice this as a growing self-awareness, a new kind of quiet honesty, a sense that something in you is becoming more real, even if you don't yet know what that something is.

Forming the Architecture of the Next Version of You

Even when you feel empty, flat, or directionless, your soul is sketching the blueprint of who you are becoming. It forms silently, through intuition, inner shifts, disinterest in old patterns, new desires, quiet visions, and unexplainable pulls. The softening of old stories. The quiet strengthening of new ones. This architecture is delicate at first — like a seed beneath soil. You can't see it yet. But you can feel something stirring.

When it is ready, it rises.

Under the surface, the in-between is fierce with creation. Even when your life feels paused, your soul is not paused. It is orchestrating your next becoming with a precision and intelligence that your mind could never engineer. You are not waiting. You are forming.

* * *

Practice: Clearing 'Not You' (3 minutes)

This is a body practice, not a visualization.

Stand or sit. Exhale through the mouth three times, like a gentle sigh. On the next exhale, let a quiet sound come if it wants to — a hum, a sigh, a soft 'ah.' Then do a simple sweep: place your hands at the top of your chest and slowly move them down your arms to your hands, as if brushing something off. Repeat two or three times.

Now place one hand on your belly and notice: What feels like yours? What feels like pressure that doesn't belong to you? No answer is required. Just notice. Let your system begin to learn the difference, without effort. Sometimes the body releases before the mind understands.

* * *

How the In-Between Ends

The in-between does not end with a revelation. It does not end with certainty or a dramatic knowing. It ends the way dawn arrives — quietly, softly, almost imperceptibly at first, and then unmistakably.

You begin to feel small, steady inner yeses. Not the loud or impulsive yes — the quiet one. A soft hum in the chest. A warming in the belly. A gentle forward tilt in the body when something is true. You feel drawn to things without needing to explain why. These small yeses are the first signs that a new orientation system is coming online. The new self doesn't arrive through force. It arrives through resonance.

Your inner world becomes more spacious. There is breathing room, less internal pressure, less urgency, less mental noise, more patience, more honesty, more neutrality. You don't feel done. You feel different. This spaciousness is the new self-making room inside you.

You start telling the truth faster. Not dramatic truth — quiet truth. Truths like: *I don't want that anymore. I think I'm done with this. This doesn't fit. I want something different. I'm not going back to that.* These truths land with a calm certainty rather than panic. This is the voice of the new self-finding its language.

You feel less attached to outcomes and more connected to alignment. You stop gripping for answers and stop forcing clarity. Instead, you find yourself asking: *Does this feel right? Does this feel true? Does this support who I'm becoming?* The future no longer feels like something to chase. It feels like something you are in relationship with.

Desire returns — gently at first, then with more clarity. During the in-between, desire often disappears, not because it's gone, but because it's reorganizing. When the new self begins to emerge, you feel tiny sparks: curiosity, interest, a pull toward something, the warmth of possibility.

Desire returns when it has finally aligned with truth. And at some point, you begin to feel yourself again — not the old self, but a truer one. Like you've come home, but to a home you've never lived in before. Like you're meeting yourself for the first time, and yet recognizing yourself deeply. The new self carries greater clarity, a softer nervous system, more natural limits, more internal spaciousness, more intuitive precision, more stability, more truth. You don't become someone new.

You become someone real.

The in-between ends the moment you can feel the next step — not the whole path, just the next step. When that step arrives, you know the passage has done its work. Not because everything is clear, but because you are.

* * *

Practice: The First Yes (2 minutes, done over a day)

The new self doesn't arrive as a big plan. It arrives as a small honest yes.

Today, look for one tiny yes that doesn't require explanation: a food your body actually wants, a walk instead of scrolling, a moment of sunlight, choosing quiet, saying no to one thing, resting without earning it. When you feel that yes, pause for five seconds. Let your body register it.

That pause is how the new self takes root. You don't need the whole path. You only need the next true step.

7

THE FIRST LIGHT:
WHEN THE NEW SELF
BEGINS TO TAKE SHAPE

Every transformation has a moment when something inside you begins to turn toward the light.

It doesn't arrive with certainty.

It doesn't announce itself with clarity.

It doesn't feel complete.

It arrives quietly.

As a breath that moves more easily than it did before.

As a softness in the body you weren't expecting.

As a moment of calm that doesn't collapse.

As a subtle sense of inner room.

As a whisper, barely audible, this feels different.

This is not the end of the threshold.

It is not the arrival of a finished self.

It is the first light.

After the unraveling.

After the in-between.

After the long season of not knowing.

Something begins to rise.

And paradoxically, this is often the phase people trust the least. Not because it is difficult, but because it is unfamiliar. When you've spent so long shedding, dissolving, releasing, and letting go, the sensation of opening can feel vulnerable. Suspicious.

Almost too quiet to be real.

You may wonder:

Is this stable?

Is this just a pause before I fall back again?

Can I trust this softness?

What if this disappears?

This chapter is here to name what is actually happening. To help you recognize the first light when it appears. To understand why it can feel both beautiful and unsteady. And to show you how to stay with what is emerging without forcing it, rushing it, or trying to define it too soon.

When Emergence Feels Both Gentle and Unsettling

Early emergence is one of the most delicate phases of becoming. It is not the beginning of the threshold — the rupture. It is not the deep middle — the in-between. It is the moment after all of that, when something inside you begins to lift its head.

This lifting is subtle. You may feel moments of ease that weren't there before. A quiet steadiness. A sense of internal alignment that doesn't need explanation. A softness replacing the tension you once carried unconsciously.

And yet, alongside the beauty, there can be a strange unsteadiness. This does not mean something is wrong. It means you are standing in a self you have never lived from before.

For a long time, your nervous system was organized around survival. Around bracing.

Around anticipating impact. Around staying ahead of disappointment. Even when that life was painful, it was familiar. The new self does not operate from those strategies. So when those protections dissolve, there can be a momentary gap — a place where the old ways are gone, and the new instincts are still forming.

This gap can feel like vulnerability.

Not because you are unsafe,

but because you are no longer armored.

Relief can feel foreign when you've lived in survival.

Softness can feel like exposure.

Ease can feel unearned.

Quiet can feel unsettling.

Your system is learning something entirely new:

I can be open and still be okay.

I can relax without collapsing.

I can feel peace without waiting for it to disappear.

This learning takes time.

How the New Self Begins to Make Itself Known

The new self does not announce itself with declarations or plans. It doesn't arrive with a clear vision of where you're headed or a confident sense of who you're becoming. It arrives far more quietly than that, through absences as much as presences. Through what you no longer feel compelled to do. Through what you no longer need to prove.

You may notice you are no longer gripping the way you used to. That old triggers still appear, but they pass more quickly. That fear still visits, but it no longer feels like truth.

That you recover faster. That you soften sooner. That you don't spiral as far.

You may find yourself less interested in conversations that once pulled you in — the circular ones, the ones that left you feeling smaller, the ones where you performed a version of yourself you've quietly outgrown. Not with judgment. Just with a settled disinterest, as if something in you has simply moved on.

You may feel more able to receive small moments of goodness — a kindness, a beauty in nature, a moment of genuine connection — without immediately deflecting them or waiting for them to be taken away. Receiving, which once felt complicated or even dangerous, begins to feel more natural. Not all the time. But more than before.

Old roles begin to feel strange in your hands. The part you played — the strong one, the accommodating one, the one who needed nothing — no longer fits the way it did. Not because you've rejected it, but because you've grown past the fear that made it necessary.

And underneath all of it, you may feel something that is difficult to name. A sense of being more yourself, even if you don't yet know who that self fully is. A quiet familiarity with your own inner landscape. A comfort in your own company that wasn't always there.

This is emergence.

It is not loud.

It is not complete.

But it is real.

The First Instincts of the New Self

Before the new self has language, it has instinct. And these instincts don't feel like decisions. They feel like gentle refusals and quiet invitations that arise before you've consciously chosen anything.

You may feel the impulse to slow down, even when nothing appears wrong. To linger a little longer in the morning before reaching for your phone. To pause before responding.

To let silence be enough.

You may feel less able to tolerate what once felt normal — overextension, noise, self-betrayal, emotional labor you were never really equipped to carry, performances of okayness that cost you more than anyone knew. This lowered tolerance is not fragility. It is honesty. Your system is no longer willing to override what it actually knows.

You may feel drawn toward simplicity — not as a philosophy or an aesthetic, but as a bodily need. Fewer things. Quieter evenings. Food that genuinely nourishes.

Conversations that feel real. The pull is almost physical, like the body leaning away from excess and toward what actually sustains it.

There is often a stronger pull toward nourishment rather than numbing. Toward truth rather than appeasement. Toward honesty rather than explanation. You find yourself less willing to say yes when you mean no. Less willing to perform enthusiasm you don't feel. Less willing to abandon your own knowing in order to keep the peace.

And you may feel a desire to protect your energy — not from a place of fear or self-protection in the old guarded sense, but from a place of care. A recognition that what you give your attention to shapes you. That your time and presence are not infinite. That choosing wisely is not self-ishness. It is a form of respect for what is forming inside you.

Alongside all of this, a quiet trust begins to emerge:

I don't know where this is going.

But I know this is real.

These instincts are not asking you to leap. They are asking you to listen. They are shaping the internal landscape so that when the outer path appears, you will be able to walk it — not because you prepared perfectly, but because you stayed honest.

When the Good Feels Hard to Trust

There is something that happens in early emergence that very few people talk about, and even fewer expect.

The good arrives — and you don't quite trust it.

A moment of ease appears and some part of you waits for it to collapse. A feeling of peace moves through you and you brace, almost involuntarily, against it. Something good happens and instead of receiving it fully, you look for the catch. You feel quiet and then worry that the quiet is wrong — that you should be doing more, feeling more, reaching for more.

This is not ingratitude. It is not pessimism. It is what happens when a nervous system has spent a long time in survival and hasn't yet learned to trust safety.

When difficulty is what you know, ease can feel like the calm before something breaks.

Softness can feel like vulnerability to harm. Goodness can feel unearned — as though you haven't suffered enough, worked hard enough, or become enough to deserve what is gently arriving.

So you may find yourself subtly pushing it away. Getting busy just as things settle.

Creating friction in moments of ease. Reaching for something to fix when nothing actually needs fixing. These are not character flaws. They are the protective self doing what it has always done — keeping you from relaxing too fully into something that might be taken away.

The invitation in this phase is not to force trust. It is to notice the bracing and gently stay anyway.

When ease arrives, let it land for a moment before you question it.

When something feels good, let yourself feel it before you explain it away.

When peace appears, let it be real, even if only for a breath.

You do not have to be certain the good will last. You only have to stop working so hard to make it leave.

The nervous system learns safety through repeated experience, not through understanding. Every time you let goodness land — even briefly, even imperfectly — you are teaching your system something essential: this is allowed. *I am allowed to be here.*

The ground holds even when I stop bracing against it.

This is slow work. It is quiet work. And it is some of the most important work of this phase.

How to Stay With What Is Emerging

The greatest risk in this phase is not stagnation. It is interference. Trying to define what is still forming. Trying to accelerate what needs time. Trying to become instead of allowing something to happen.

There is a particular kind of impatience that arises in early emergence — a wanting to know what this all means, to name the new self, to announce the change, to skip ahead to the part where you feel sure. The mind, having waited through the long uncertainty of the in-between, is ready for answers. It wants the new chapter to begin.

But the new self doesn't strengthen through intensity. It strengthens through consistency. Through small acts of truth repeated over time. Through choosing alignment over urgency, again and again, in the small moments that no one else sees. This is not a time to assess your progress. It is a time to let the roots grow unseen. What nourishes you now matters. What drains you now matters. Your system will tell you — through expansion or contraction, through ease or tightness, through resonance or the quiet collapse that happens when something isn't right.

Listen.

Let goodness land without bracing.

Let joy appear without suspicion.

Let rest be part of the medicine.

The new self does not grow through pressure.

It grows through permission.

Walking While the New Self Is Still Tender

Early emergence is a bridge. You are not meant to live here forever, but you are meant to walk it carefully. There is a temptation in this phase to move quickly — to take the new self out into the world, to test it, to prove it. But tenderness asks for a different pace.

Move at the pace of your breath. Respond more slowly than you used to. Notice when you are about to override something quiet inside you and pause there, even briefly, before you decide.

Protect your inner space without isolating yourself. This is a balance worth holding. The new self needs shelter to form — less exposure to environments that require the old performance, less time in conversations that pull you back into familiar roles. But isolation can become its own form of avoidance. The new self also needs contact — real contact, with people who can meet you where you actually are.

Share selectively. Not because your experience is too precious to be spoken, but because it is still tender, and tender things need the right conditions to be received. Not everyone in your life will have the capacity to hold what you are moving through. That is not their failure. It is simply information about where to bring your most vulnerable truths.

Choose environments that support truth. Notice how different spaces feel in your body — which rooms, which conversations, which routines leave you feeling more your-self afterward, and which ones require you to contract. This is not about perfection. It is about paying attention to what the emerging self can and cannot yet sustain.

When tiredness appears, let it be rest, not regression.

When fear appears, meet it without letting it lead.

When joy appears, welcome it.

This is how the new self stabilizes —

not by hardening,

but by rooting.

* * *

Practice: Letting It Land (2 minutes)

This is for the moments when something good arrives and you notice yourself bracing against it or moving away from it before it can settle.

When ease, relief, joy, or quiet appears, pause. Place one hand on your chest.

Take one slow breath in and let the exhale be long.

Then say, silently or aloud: This is allowed. Let your body hear that. Not as a command, but as a permission. Repeat it once more if you need to.

Notice what happens — even a small softening, a slight drop in the shoulders, a breath that lands a little deeper. That is your system beginning to learn that the good is safe to receive.

You don't have to stay long. Even ten seconds of letting something good land without bracing is enough to begin rewiring what safety feels like.

* * *

When Life Begins to Respond

As the new self settles, life begins to answer. Quietly. A conversation opens. An opportunity arrives without force. A desire clarifies. An old attachment loosens. A next step becomes visible — not the whole path, just one step.

This is how emergence moves into form. You do not need the full map. You only need to recognize the opening in front of you.

The new chapter of your life does not begin with certainty.

It begins with response.

A soft yes.

A gentle step.

A willingness to trust what is already rising.

This is the first light.

And it is enough to walk by.

8

WHEN LIFE BEGINS
TO ANSWER BACK

There is a moment after a threshold when you realize something subtle but unmistakable:

Life is responding to you differently.

Not dramatically.

Not all at once.

But in quiet, precise ways that feel almost conversational, as if the world is saying, "I see the shift you've made."

This is not because you did something right.

It's because you became available.

When the inner architecture changes, life doesn't rush in to reward you. It reorganizes, slowly, intelligently, to meet the version of you that now exists. This chapter is about recognizing that moment. And learning how to walk it without forcing, doubting, or collapsing back into old ways of relating to the world.

When the Outer World Begins to Move

After a threshold, the first outer changes are rarely the ones you expect. They don't arrive as big decisions or dramatic endings. They don't come wrapped in certainty or announced with fanfare. They arrive much more quietly than that, and because of their quietness, they are easy to miss.

A conversation that once left you feeling contracted ends differently. You notice you said something true that you might have softened before, and the other person received it. A dynamic you once managed carefully — monitoring your words, anticipating reactions, making yourself smaller to keep the peace — simply loses its pull. You are still in the same relationship, the same room, the same exchange. But something in how you inhabit it has shifted.

An opportunity arrives that doesn't come with the familiar tightening in your chest. No pressure to prove yourself, no urgency to secure it before it disappears, no sense that you need to override your own hesitation to say yes. It simply appears, unhurried and spacious, and you find yourself curious rather than anxious about it.

These are the first signs. They are easy to overlook because they are subtle, and because we are conditioned to look for change in the dramatic and visible. But life reorganizes from the inside out. The outer shifts follow the inner ones. And the outer shifts, at first, look less like new chapters and more like the quiet resolution of old ones.

Life begins to mirror your internal steadiness — not because the world has changed, but because you are no longer moving through it from survival. You are no longer bracing.

And the world, meeting less resistance, begins to move differently around you.

The Four Ways Life Responds

The reorganization that follows a threshold tends to move through four distinct shifts.

They don't arrive in a tidy sequence — they often overlap and weave through one another. But over time, each one becomes recognizable.

The first is that what no longer fits begins to fall away without effort. This is often the quietest sign and the one most likely to be mistaken for loss. Things that once required constant managing — relationships held together by performance, roles maintained through self-suppression, commitments that slowly drained you — begin to loosen on their own. You don't have to force endings. You don't have to manufacture closure or build a case for why something needs to change. You simply stop investing energy where it no longer belongs, and the thing naturally recedes.

The old self needed effort to stay in misalignment. The new self doesn't. When you stop holding something in place that doesn't fit, it drifts. And what remains — the relationships, the work, the commitments that do belong — tends to feel more solid, more reciprocal, more real.

The second shift is that opportunities arrive without urgency. This is one of the most distinct and recognizable changes. Before, when something appeared that seemed like it might matter — a door opening, a possibility emerging — there was often an anxious quality to it. A sense that you had to decide quickly, prove yourself worthy, reach for it before it disappeared. The opportunity felt like a test.

Aligned opportunities feel different. They arrive with a kind of patience. They don't demand that you override your body or abandon your limits to say yes. There is curiosity in them rather than pressure, possibility rather than obligation. They invite rather than demand. And they tend to stay — they don't evaporate the moment you don't immediately leap. If something requires you to betray your own timing to secure it, that is information. If something holds while you take a breath and listen, that is also information.

The third shift is that discernment becomes embodied rather than mental. For a long time, the question was: *Is this right? Does this make sense? What should I do?* These are mind questions, and they look for mind answers. But the new self doesn't navigate this way. It navigates through the body — through what settles the breath and what tightens it, through what feels clean and what feels heavy, through what you can remain present with and what immediately pulls you out of yourself.

You may notice this happening before you consciously recognize it as a new way of knowing. You decline something and realize only afterward that your body had already answered before your mind caught up. You feel drawn toward something without being able to fully explain why, and the pull turns out to be trustworthy. This is discernment living in contact rather than analysis. It is quieter than the old way, and more accurate.

The fourth shift is that you begin to respond rather than chase. The old self pursued —chased answers, chased certainty, chased signs that it was moving in the right direction. The new self recognizes openings. It notices what appears repeatedly without being forced. It pays attention to what stays when you stop pushing. It trusts what returns after rest. And it meets what comes halfway rather than running ahead of it.

This is not passivity. It is a different quality of engagement — one that arises from trust rather than fear, from presence rather than urgency. Life at this stage doesn't require effort so much as it requires responsiveness. The willingness to notice, to receive, to say yes or no from a place of genuine knowing.

The Difference Between Alignment and Impulse

This is where many people stumble — not because they have lost their way, but because alignment and impulse can feel deceptively similar in the body, especially at first.

Impulse tends to arrive with urgency. There is a charge to it, an excited anxiety, a sense that you must decide now or lose the chance. It often carries a story — about what this opportunity means, about what it will finally give you, about how it will resolve something that has been unresolved for too long. Impulse disguises itself as excitement, but underneath it there is often a reaching quality, a grasping. It can feel like relief because it seems to offer an escape from the discomfort of not knowing. But it doesn't usually quiet the nervous system. It stimulates it.

Alignment feels different. It is steadier. It doesn't spike and it doesn't demand. There is a calm quality to it even when it is also exciting — a sense that the yes or no arising in you has roots, that it comes from somewhere real. You can breathe while considering it. Your body doesn't contract around it. It may ask something of you, but it doesn't ask you to abandon yourself to say yes.

If you have to convince yourself, pause.

If you can breathe while considering it, listen more closely.

The clearest test is this: does it ask you to override what you know? Alignment never requires self-betrayal. It may ask for courage — to step into something unfamiliar, to trust something not yet fully formed. But it does not ask you to leave yourself behind in order to move forward.

How to Walk Forward Without Collapsing Into Overthinking

At this stage, the mind may want to reassert itself. After the long uncertainty of the in-between, after all that trusting without knowing, the mind is ready to take the wheel again. It wants to plan, to decide, to name the new identity, to figure out the shape of the next chapter.

This impulse is understandable. And it doesn't need to be fought. It only needs to be gently redirected.

You do not need to decide your future right now. You do not need to explain your change to the people around you or find language that makes the shift legible to everyone in your life. You do not need to commit to a path before you can feel where it leads. What is being asked of you at this stage is simpler and more immediate than any of that.

Respond honestly to what is in front of you. Move when it feels supported. Pause when your body asks. Stay in relationship with yourself — checking in, noticing, adjusting.

This is not small. It is, in fact, the whole practice.

Life will not punish you for slowness here. It will meet you in it. The ground that has been forming beneath you through all the months of inner work is real. It holds. You don't have to rush to prove that it does.

What Expands Next

The expansion that follows a threshold is rarely external first. The outer life reorganizes, but only after something deeper has shifted — and that deeper shift is what you are living in right now.

What expands first is your capacity. The ability to hold more truth without contracting. To stay present in difficult conversations without disappearing. To receive goodness without bracing. To tolerate uncertainty without manufacturing false resolution. These expansions are invisible to anyone watching, but you feel them — in the moments when you would once have collapsed and instead you simply stay.

What expands alongside capacity is trust — in your own timing, in your own body's knowing, in the intelligence of the process you've been walking. Not a blind trust, not a performed optimism, but a quiet and earned confidence in your ability to navigate whatever comes. You have already walked through things you didn't know how to walk through. That knowledge lives in you now. It doesn't leave.

From this expansion, life reorganizes naturally. Not all at once. Not in ways you can always predict or plan for. But with an accuracy that becomes recognizable over time — a sense that what is arriving belongs, that what is falling away was ready to go, that the life taking shape around you is closer to the truth of who you actually are.

* * *

Practice: The Noticing (done over a day)

This is not a sitting practice. It is a practice of attention woven through ordinary moments.

Today, notice once — just once — when life meets you in a small way you might otherwise have missed. It might be a conversation that lands differently. An opportunity that arrives without pressure. A moment when you respond from a new place and feel it in your body. A door that opens without effort.

When you notice it, pause for five seconds. Place a hand on your chest.

Let yourself register that this is happening. Say quietly: I see this.

You don't need to analyze it or make meaning of it right away. You only need to acknowledge it. Life is beginning to answer back. The practice is simply learning to hear it.

* * *

A Quiet Truth to Carry Forward

You are not being tested now.

You are being met.

Life is not asking you to leap.

It is asking you to notice where the ground already holds you.

And as you learn to walk from this place — not rushing, not explaining, not collapsing — the next chapter begins to form beneath your feet.

9

WHEN THE NEW SELF
BEGINS TO ROOT

There is a quiet phase after emergence that few people talk about.

The threshold has been crossed.

The in-between has completed its work.

The first light has risen.

And yet — life does not suddenly look different.

This is often where confusion returns. Not because something has gone wrong, but because something subtler is happening. The new self is no longer arriving. It is rooting.

Rooting is not dramatic.

It does not announce itself with certainty or clarity or visible change.

It happens the way roots always do —

beneath the surface, out of sight,

strengthening what will later hold weight.

This chapter is about that phase. The phase where you are no longer unraveling, but you are not yet fully living from the new self either. The phase where the inner truth is real but not fully reflected in the outer world.

This is not delay.

It is integration.

Why Life May Look the Same Even Though You Are Not

One of the most disorienting experiences in transformation is the gap between inner change and outer evidence. You feel different — genuinely, unmistakably different — and yet you wake up in the same home, move through the same routines, sit across from the same people. Nothing on the outside announces what has happened on the inside. And in that gap, doubt can move in quietly.

Did anything really happen?

Did I imagine that shift?

If I've changed, why hasn't my life?

This doubt is understandable. But it misreads what is

happening. Rooting always comes before restructuring. The inner system must stabilize before the outer world can safely reorganize around it. If life changed too quickly — if relationships shifted, circumstances rearranged, and new chapters opened — before the new self had sufficient strength to hold them, the transformation would collapse under its own weight. The outer life would arrive before there was enough of you to meet it.

So instead, something quieter and more essential occurs. You begin responding differently inside the same life. The same conversation, but you say something true where you once stayed silent. The same relationship, but you hold a limit you once let dissolve. The same moment of stress, but you return to yourself more quickly than before. Nothing visible has changed. But the quality of how you inhabit your life has changed completely.

This is where real embodiment begins. Not in the new chapter, but in the living of this one — more honestly, more steadily, more like yourself than you have been in a long time.

What Rooting Actually Feels Like

Rooting does not feel like excitement or momentum. It does not feel like arrival. It doesn't have the quality of breakthrough or revelation. If anything, it can feel almost unremarkable — which is precisely why it is so easy to underestimate.

It feels like steadiness without certainty. A kind of groundedness that doesn't require you to know what comes next in order to trust that you can meet it. It feels like presence without urgency — the ability to be in a moment fully, without needing to immediately move to the next one. It feels like clarity without language — a knowing in the body that hasn't yet found its words but is real and reliable nonetheless.

You may notice you pause where you once reacted. That a comment which would once have pulled you off center lands differently now — still felt, but not destabilizing. You may find yourself sensing truth sooner in your body, before your mind has assembled the analysis. You say less, but what you say carries more weight. You feel less compelled to explain yourself, to justify your choices, to make your inner life legible to everyone around you.

You may also notice that you tolerate less misalignment — not through drama or conflict, but through a quiet refusal that arises almost on its own. Things that once felt tolerable simply stop feeling that way. Not because you have become demanding, but because something in you has become more honest. The new self knows what fits and what doesn't, and it is increasingly unwilling to pretend otherwise.

These are not small changes. They are structural. They are the nervous system learning, slowly and through repetition, that this new way of being is not a temporary state but a permanent one.

This is who we are now.

Ordinary Life as the Practice

Rooting does not happen in retreat or in ceremony or in the quiet of a dedicated practice. It happens in the grocery store. In the difficult phone call. In the moment you almost say yes out of habit and catch yourself. In the morning when you choose to sit with your breath instead of immediately reaching for distraction. In the conversation where you tell a small truth you would once have smoothed over.

This is what integration looks like from the inside — not a series of spiritual experiences, but a series of ordinary moments in which the new self shows up and holds. A meeting where you speak from your actual experience instead of performing competence. A friendship where you ask for what you need instead of pretending you don't need anything. An evening where you rest without earning it first.

The insight work is largely complete. You have already understood enough. You have already felt enough, released enough, dissolved enough old patterns to know what is true in you. What the rooting phase asks of you now is simpler and in some ways more demanding than any of that: to live what you know, in the small moments, when no one is watching, when there is no particular reason to choose differently except that it is honest.

Integration happens when you choose truth in small moments without making a production of it. When you honor your limits without justifying them at length. When you rest when your body asks rather than when you feel you have finally earned it. When you speak honestly without the paragraph of explanation that used to follow every true thing you said.

These are not spiritual practices. They are ways of being. And the repetition of them — day after day, in the unremarkable fabric of an ordinary life — is what makes the new self real. Not as an experience, but as a home.

Why Old Patterns Still Appear and Why That Is Not Failure

During rooting, old patterns sometimes return. Not with the same intensity — not the full force of what they once carried — but with a familiarity that can be alarming. You recognize the contraction, the impulse, the old voice. And you wonder: *why is this still here? Shouldn't it be gone by now?*

It returns because the system is checking. Not because the work has failed, but because the nervous system is thorough. It is asking, quietly and beneath the level of conscious thought: *do we still need this strategy? Is this pattern still required for safety? Can we let it go now, or does it still serve something?*

Each time the old pattern arises and you stay present with it — without collapsing into it, without white-knuckling your way through it, but simply remaining — something completes. The system gets an answer. The pattern loosens a little more of its authority. Not because you defeated it, but because you demonstrated, once again, that you no longer need it to survive.

You don't need to eliminate the pattern. You only need to stop organizing your identity around it. Rooting happens not when old patterns disappear, but when they lose their claim on who you are. When they become something you notice rather than something you become.

The Quiet of Having Nothing Left to Prove

One of the most unexpected hallmarks of rooting is a growing quiet. Not the quiet of disconnection or withdrawal, but the quiet of completion. A sense that something that once needed constant tending no longer does.

You may find yourself less drawn to talk about what you've been through. Less interested in finding the right words to make your transformation visible or legible to the people around you. Less compelled to be understood — by friends, by family, by the various parts of your life that haven't shifted at the same pace you have.

This is not indifference. It is not disconnection from the people you love. It is something closer to sovereignty — an increasing trust in your own inner reference point that no longer requires external confirmation to feel real. The truth you have arrived at doesn't need to be spoken to be true. It doesn't need an audience to be valid. It doesn't need other people's understanding in order to hold.

There is something quietly revolutionary about this. For most of us, what we know about ourselves has been shaped, in part, by how others have reflected us back. We have depended on being seen to feel real. We have needed the understanding of those close to us to trust our own experience. And while being witnessed remains meaningful, rooting brings with it a kind of inner witnessing that doesn't need to be supplemented from the outside.

When truth is embodied, it no longer needs narration.

You may still choose to share your experience — with people who have the capacity to receive it, in moments that feel right. But the sharing comes from fullness now, not from need. From the desire for genuine connection, not from the anxiety of being misunderstood. That distinction, quiet as it is, marks a profound shift in how you move through relationship.

Patience With the Pace of Outer Change

This is perhaps the hardest part of rooting to navigate, and the one where people most often lose faith in the process.

The inner work feels real. The shift is genuine. And yet the outer life — the relationships, the circumstances, the material conditions of your days — hasn't reorganized to match it yet. You are living a new truth inside a life that was built for an older one. And that gap, which can stretch for weeks or months, can feel like evidence that nothing has actually changed.

It isn't. It is evidence that the outer world moves more slowly than the inner one.

Always. The inner self reorganizes first, and the outer life follows — but on its own timeline, and not on command.

Outer change comes after stability, not before. If relationships began reorganizing before you were rooted enough to hold the new dynamic, they would overwhelm the very ground you're trying to establish. If new opportunities arrived before your capacity had expanded enough to receive them steadily, they would activate the old survival responses rather than the new ones. The timing that feels like delay is actually protection. Life is waiting until what it sends can be met with the full strength of who you are becoming.

What is asked of you during this gap is something both simple and genuinely difficult: to keep living from the new truth even while the outer life hasn't yet caught up. To make choices from the new self even when the circumstances around you still reflect the old one. To trust the roots that are forming beneath you even though you cannot yet see what they will hold.

This is quiet, unglamorous, faithful work. It doesn't look like transformation from the outside. It often doesn't feel particularly spiritual from the inside. It just feels like living honestly, again and again, in ordinary moments. And that faithfulness — that continued choosing of truth in the small moments — is what makes the outer change possible when it finally arrives.

The Body as the Final Integrator

During rooting, the body becomes the primary guide once more. Not the mind's analysis of what is happening, not the spiritual framework you've been walking within, but the direct, immediate, lived experience of your own physical presence.

You may notice a particular kind of fatigue — not the exhaustion of the in-between, but a settling tiredness, as if your system is finally laying something down. A desire for simplicity, for grounded routine, for the same nourishing things at the same reliable times. Less tolerance for excess, for overstimulation, for the kind of busyness that once served as useful distraction. A pull toward quiet consistency that feels less like withdrawal and more like preference.

This is consolidation. The body is anchoring the new self into muscle, breath, posture, rhythm, and instinctive response. Every time you pause before reacting, the body learns that pause. Every time you rest when asked, the body learns that rest is safe. Every time you speak from truth rather than from performance, the body learns what truth feels like as a physical state. Slowly, steadily, the new self becomes not just something you believe in or aspire to, but something you are — in the most literal, physical, cellular sense of the word.

This is how truth becomes stable. Not through understanding, but through the body living it, again and again, until it is no longer an achievement but simply a way of being.

* * *

Practice: The Small Faithful Moment (done throughout the day)

Rooting is built in small moments, not large ones. This practice asks you to choose one small act of truth today — not because it is meaningful, but simply because it is honest.

It might be resting when you feel tired instead of pushing through. Speaking a quiet preference instead of deferring. Pausing before you respond to something that would once have pulled you off center. Saying no to something small that doesn't fit. Saying yes to something small that does.

When you do it, notice your body's response. Not to analyze it — just to feel it. A small easing. A subtle sense of alignment. The quiet satisfaction of having been true to yourself in a moment when it would have been easy not to be.

This is rooting. Not the dramatic gesture, but the faithful repetition of small honest choices, accumulated over time, until they become the ground you stand on.

* * *

How to Know Rooting Is Happening

You will know not because everything feels clear, but because something has become quiet in a way it wasn't before. You trust yourself more than you trust your fear. You feel steadier even in uncertainty — not unmoved by it, but no longer undone by it. You no longer need to be convinced that the shift is real. You sense alignment without requiring excitement to confirm it.

You feel quieter.

But more real.

The life forming around you may not yet look like what you imagined. The outer changes may still be arriving slowly, partially, in ways that don't fully satisfy the mind's desire for visible evidence. But something underneath has solidified. Something that was fragile has become sturdy. Something that was forming has formed.

This Is the Phase Where Becoming Turns Into Living

Thresholds initiate change.

The in-between dissolves the old.

Emergence introduces the new.

But rooting is where becoming becomes a life.

This is where truth stops being an experience and starts being how you move through the world.

You are not meant to rush this phase.

You are meant to inhabit it.

Because once the roots are strong,

the next expansion will not destabilize you.

It will feel like home.

10
WHEN THE WORLD
BEGINS TO RESPOND

There is a moment, often subtle, when you realize something has shifted beyond you.

Not because you decided anything.

Not because you announced a change.

Not because you tried to manifest or orchestrate.

But because life begins to meet you differently.

This chapter is not about doing anything new.

It is about recognizing what is already happening.

When External Change Follows Internal Truth

Life does not respond to intention alone. It responds to coherence — to the alignment between what you carry inside and how you move through the world. When those two things finally match, something changes in the quality of your presence. Not dramatically. Not in ways that are easy to point to. But in ways that other people feel, that circumstances begin to reflect, and that you yourself begin to notice with a quiet astonishment.

This is not alignment magic. It is not the universe rewarding your growth or delivering what you've earned. It is something more practical and more honest than that. When your nervous system stabilizes, when your truth becomes embodied, when your limits become implicit rather than performed, the energy you bring into every room and every exchange is different. Less defended. Less contradictory. Less divided against itself. And the world, which is far more sensitive to these shifts than we are typically taught to believe, begins to move differently in response.

People relate to you differently — not always because they understand what has changed, but because something in how you occupy your own space has shifted.

Opportunities arrive that feel genuinely fitting rather than merely possible. Old dynamics that once required constant management begin to lose their grip, not through confrontation but through a quiet withdrawal of the energy that kept them alive. Decisions that once felt agonizing become simpler because you are no longer deciding from two different versions of yourself simultaneously.

This reorganization is not about the world finally giving you what you deserve. It is about you finally being available to receive what was already there. The threshold clears what was blocking the connection between you and the life that belongs to you. What follows is less a reward than a reunion.

The Experience of Being Seen

There is something that happens in this phase that can be as disorienting as it is welcome: you become visible in a new way.

For a long time — perhaps for most of your life — some part of you has been hidden. Not deliberately, not dishonestly, but structurally. The old self, shaped by survival and adaptation, occupied space in a particular way. Careful. Managed. Aware, always, of how it was being perceived. It knew how to move through rooms and relationships with just enough of itself showing to stay connected, but not so much that it risked the exposure that once felt dangerous.

Rooting changes this. When the new self has taken hold — when you are no longer bracing, no longer divided, no longer running two selves simultaneously — something in your presence opens. You are no longer buffered by confusion or protected by contraction. You are simply there, more fully than before, and the world can feel it.

This visibility can feel exhilarating. There is something deeply relieving about being met as you actually are, rather than as the careful version of yourself you once presented.

Conversations go deeper more quickly. People say things to you they don't usually say. You are trusted with more, invited into more, seen as capable of more than you may have anticipated.

And it can also feel, at moments, intensely vulnerable.

When you have spent years behind a careful presentation, being genuinely seen — even when it is welcome, even when it is kind — can activate old fears. The fear of being too much. The fear that what people are responding to will somehow disappoint them when they see further. The fear that the visibility will bring not belonging but scrutiny. These fears don't mean you are wrong to be more open. They mean the nervous system is encountering something unfamiliar, and it is doing what nervous systems do — checking whether it is safe.

What steadies you here is not certainty that you will be received perfectly. It is the knowledge that you can survive being seen. That you are no longer dependent on others' understanding to know what is true in you. That being misread or misunderstood, while still uncomfortable, is no longer the threat it once was. You have an inner reference point now that doesn't require external confirmation to hold.

Life can now see you.

And you are strong enough to let it.

When the World Still Doesn't Fully Match

Even in this phase, the outer world does not always reorganize completely or quickly. A door cracks open but doesn't yet swing wide. A connection appears but unfolds slowly, over months rather than days. A path reveals itself one step at a time, and the next step only becomes visible after you've taken the one before it.

This is not withholding. It is pacing. Life moves at the speed your nervous system can sustain, and what arrives in this phase tends to arrive at a rate you can actually integrate. This is a form of care, even when it feels like frustration.

There may also be places in your life that are slower to reorganize than others. A relationship that has known you for decades and holds a particular image of who you were. A professional context that still relates to the old version of your capabilities. A family system that has its own investment in the person you've been. These reorganize more slowly not because change isn't real, but because other people and systems need time to update their understanding of you — just as you needed time to update your understanding of yourself.

Your work here is not to push or to prove. It is to continue responding honestly from the new self, even in the contexts that haven't yet caught up. Every interaction in which you show up as you actually are — rather than contracting back into the old familiar shape — teaches the world around you who you are now. This is quiet, patient, faithful work. And it is enough.

What Quiet Confidence Actually Feels Like

There is a particular quality that begins to form in this phase that is worth naming, because it doesn't feel like what most people imagine confidence to feel like.

It doesn't feel like certainty. It doesn't feel like having answers, or knowing exactly where you're headed, or feeling assured that things will work out in the specific way you hope. It doesn't feel loud or expansive or particularly notice-able from the inside.

It feels like a kind of settledness in the body. A sense of being at home in your own skin that doesn't require a particular circumstance to sustain it. You wake up and you are simply here — not bracing for what the day might require of you, not running a quiet inventory of how you measure up, not managing the distance between who you are and who you think you should be.

You find that you are no longer afraid of yourself in the way you once were. The inner landscape that once felt like unpre-dictable territory — where difficult emotions might surface without warning, where old patterns might pull you off course, where you might say or feel something that alarmed you — has become familiar. Not because it is always peace-ful, but because you know how to be in it. You know how to stay.

You trust your no. Not as a performance of boundaries, not as something you've learned to say because you should, but as a genuine response that arises from your actual experience of what fits and what doesn't. And you trust your yes in the same way — not as obligation or accommodation, but as real, felt desire.

You trust your ability to course-correct. This may be the deepest shift of all. You are no longer trying to get everything right the first time, to make choices so perfectly that you never have to revisit them. You trust that if you move in a direction that turns out not to be right, you will know it — your body will tell you — and you will adjust. The path is no longer something that must be perfectly foreseen. It is something you navigate in real time, with the full intelligence of who you now are.

You stop needing guarantees.

This is not because you have become fearless. It is because you have become trustworthy — to yourself. And that, quietly and completely, changes everything.

How to Walk Forward Without Collapsing Backward

Even here, at this stage of the journey, there will be moments when the pull toward the old self returns. A stressful circumstance that activates old coping. A relationship that seems to expect the previous version of you. A moment of doubt so familiar it almost feels like home.

These moments are not evidence of failure. They are evidence of how deeply the old patterns were wired, and how much repetition it takes to fully replace them. The difference now is that you recognize them sooner. You return to yourself more quickly.

The old pattern arises, and instead of becoming it, you simply notice it — and choose again.

The most important orientation at this stage remains simple: do not abandon your body for possibility. When something arrives that looks like what you've been waiting for — an opportunity, a relationship, a door opening — stay in your body as you consider it. Notice whether it settles your breath or quickens it with anxiety. Notice whether it asks you to expand into more of who you are, or to contract into less. Notice whether you can remain present with it, or whether it immediately pulls you out of yourself.

Stay rooted.

Move slowly.

Let clarity arrive after contact, not before.

Truth does not demand self-betrayal. If something requires you to override your body, betray your limits, or perform a certainty you don't actually feel in order to say yes — it is not aligned, no matter how promising it appears. The new self knows this. Trust it.

* * *

Practice: Being Here (3 minutes)

This practice is for the moments when visibility feels like too much — when being more fully seen activates old fear, or when the world responding to you more directly than before feels overwhelming rather than welcome.

Sit down somewhere quiet. Feel the weight of your body in the chair, your feet on the floor, the simple fact of your own presence in this moment. Take three slow breaths and let each exhale be longer than the inhale.

Then say, quietly: I am allowed to be seen. Let the words land in your body rather than just your mind. Notice where they meet resistance, and where they meet relief. Both are information.

You don't need to resolve the discomfort. You only need to stay present with it long enough for your system to learn: being visible is survivable. Being known is safe. The ground holds even when others can see me standing on it.

* * *

The Quiet Confidence That Emerges

What is forming in you now is not excitement. It is something quieter and more durable than that.

It is trust.

Trust in your timing.

Trust in your capacity.

Trust in your no.

Trust in your yes.

Trust in your ability to course-correct.

You stop needing guarantees.

This is how becoming turns into a life.

FINAL CHAPTER - LIVING
FROM WHAT YOU NOW KNOW

There comes a point when the work no longer asks to be named.

Not because it isn't happening,

but because it has moved beneath language.

You no longer wake asking, "*What is happening to me?*"

You wake sensing, "*I am here.*"

Something has settled.

Not into certainty,

but into truth.

You Are No Longer Searching the Way You Once Did

There was a time when you looked for yourself everywhere — in understanding, in healing, in answers, in insight, in clarity, in the future. The search had an urgency to it.

A sense that if you could just find the right key, the right teacher, the right moment of clarity, something would finally click into place and you would arrive.

But now, something is different.

You still listen.

You still feel.

You still change.

But you are no longer reaching away from yourself to do it.

You are listening from within.

This is how you know the threshold has done its work. Not because the searching has ended — curiosity and growth will always be part of who you are — but because the searching no longer feels like desperation. It feels like interest. Like genuine, unhurried inquiry into a life you are actually inhabiting rather than trying to enter.

What Has Changed Without You Forcing It

You may not be able to list what is different — but you can feel it.

You pause more naturally.

You tell the truth sooner.

You leave situations earlier.

You stay present longer.

You trust your body faster.

You stop explaining yourself so much.

You stop overriding quiet knowing.

You don't feel finished.

You feel inhabited.

This is not a small thing. To feel inhabited — to sense yourself present in your own life rather than observing it from a careful distance — is the very thing that the threshold was moving you toward all along. Not a better version of yourself. Not an arrived, resolved, complete self. But a self that is genuinely here, genuinely honest, genuinely alive to what each moment actually contains.

Life No Longer Feels Like Something You're Trying to Enter

Before, it may have felt like standing outside your own life — waiting for readiness, waiting for permission, waiting for the clarity that would finally make it safe to begin. There was always something not quite ready. Something that needed to be resolved first. Something that had to be understood before you could fully inhabit what was already yours.

Now, life meets you where you are.

You don't need the whole map.

You don't need the outcome.

You don't need to be sure.

You know how to stay.

And because you know how to stay, you can move.

Thresholds Will Still Come — But They Will Not Unmake You

This is important to understand. Threshold work does not remove future thresholds. It gives you a way to meet them without losing yourself.

There will still be moments of uncertainty, grief, fear, expansion, change, and release.

The landscape of a human life does not become smooth. It deepens. And the deepening continues to ask things of you

— courage, honesty, presence, the willingness to stay with yourself when the ground shifts again.

But now, when those moments come, something in you remains. You do not disappear. You do not abandon yourself. You do not panic at the unknown the way you once did. You recognize the language. You have walked this territory before, and your body remembers the way through.

The next threshold will not find you where this one did. It will find someone who knows how to stay.

You Are No Longer Trying to Become Someone Else

The deepest transformation in this work is this:

You stop trying to arrive somewhere.

You stop chasing a better version of yourself.

You stop negotiating your worth.

You stop postponing your life.

You live from what is already true.

And paradoxically, that is when life begins to unfold more fully. Not because you finally got it right, but because you stopped withholding yourself from it. The life waiting for you was never behind the next achievement, the next healing, the next version of yourself. It was always here, available to the degree that you were willing to show up honestly inside it.

What It Means to Live From Here

Living from here does not mean having answers. It does not mean being healed forever, or fearless, or certain, or spiritually done. It does not mean the work is finished or that the path has been fully revealed.

It means something quieter and more sustainable than any of that.

You listen before you move.

You feel before you decide.

You stay when things are tender.

You leave when something is untrue.

You rest when your body asks.

You trust when something opens.

You live in contact.

Not perfectly. Not without difficulty. But honestly, and from the inside — which is the only place a life can truly be lived from.

That is enough.

That has always been enough.

EPILOGUE — THE THRESHOLD YOU CARRY NOW

There is a moment at the end of every journey when the path grows quiet again.

Not because nothing is happening, but because what was once outside you now lives within.

You have walked through these pages, yes, but more importantly, something has been walking *within* you as you read.

Listening.

Softening.

Reorienting.

Learning how to stay.

The most important part of this book is not what you can remember or explain.

It is the subtle way your inner world has shifted while you weren't trying to change it. The way your body has begun to trust that it can be met.

Thresholds do not end when insight arrives.

They complete themselves when insight becomes a way of being.

And now, as you stand at the edge of these pages and the beginning of whatever comes next, you may notice something different in your field, not dramatic, but real.

A steadier breath.

A quieter listening.

A deeper trust in what your body knows.

A sense that your life is not random, even when it is uncertain and perhaps a subtle awareness that support exists even when it cannot be named.

You may still feel doubt.

You may still feel fear.

You may still be in the in-between.

None of that means you are doing this wrong.

Thresholds do not require you to be finished.

They only ask that you stay.

You have learned that the path does not reveal itself all at once.

It reveals itself as you become someone who can walk it.

You have learned that your body is not a problem to solve, but a guide that speaks in sensation, rhythm, and timing.

That the younger parts of you are not obstacles, but companions asking for presence rather than correction.

That change does not come when you feel ready; it comes when you are willing to remain honest.

And perhaps most importantly, you have learned this: that thresholds ask for presence and courage, not heroics, not certainty, not force, but the courage to stay with yourself when the ground shifts.

What happens next belongs to you.

Maybe you will take a small step.

Maybe you will rest.

Maybe you will notice something you have been quietly avoiding.

Maybe you will tell yourself a truth you have never spoken aloud.

Maybe you will choose differently — not because you should, but because something in you is ready.

Whatever comes, you will not meet it as the person who opened this book.

Something in you has already turned toward what is true. And when the next threshold arrives, as it always does, you will recognize it.

Not as a cliff to leap from, but as a place to stand.

To breathe.

To listen.

To stay.

Because now you know:

You are not lost in the truth.

You are being shaped by it.

CLOSING INVOCATION

A Blessing for the One Who Is Becoming

As you reach the final page of this book,

may you feel the quiet shift inside you,

the place that knows

you are standing at a beginning,

not an ending.

May your breath soften.

May your body rest.

May your heart feel spacious

enough for what is leaving

and open enough

for what is arriving.

May the thresholds in your life

not frighten you,

but invite you.

May you learn to listen

to the body's small signals,

the soul's subtle pulls,

the truths that arrive

not as lightning

but as a gentle turning

inside the chest.

May you walk tenderly

with the parts of you

still learning to trust.

May you companion

the younger selves

who once had to protect you,

and honor them

by living now

from a deeper center.

May you remember

that you do not need

the whole path

to take a true step.

May your steps be honest.

May your pace be kind.

May your choices reflect

who you are becoming,

not who you were taught to be.

May you feel supported

by the earth beneath you,

by the lineage behind you,

by the life that wishes to meet you,

and by the truth growing within you

like roots,

like breath,

like dawn.

May you stand in your becoming

with humility,

with curiosity,

and with quiet courage.

And when the next doorway appears,

as it surely will,

may you recognize it

not by how it looks,

but by how your body eases

and your soul expands

in its presence.

You are not walking

into the unknown.

You are walking

into yourself.

May this knowing

walk with you,

hold you,

and guide you

in every step ahead.

ACKNOWLEDGMENTS

To those who have walked beside me in visible and invisible ways: my teachers, my friends, my clients, and the many souls who trusted me with their stories, their thresholds, and their becoming.

Your courage shaped what this work could become.

To those who listened when I was quiet, who reflected truth back to me when I couldn't yet see it, and who honored the moments I needed to turn inward, thank you.

To the land, the sacred places, the ancestors, and the unseen presences that steady the path, your guidance continues to move through this work.

And to every person who opens these pages and meets their own unraveling with honesty and heart, you are part of this work now.

May it meet you where you are and walk with you as you become.

ABOUT THE AUTHOR

Susan H. Harris is an intuitive guide, channel, and seer whose work is rooted in presence, deep listening, and the body's innate intelligence. She works with people in moments of transition, when something within has begun to shift, but the outer life has not yet caught up.

Her approach is gentle and grounded, shaped by the understanding that real transformation does not happen through force or insight alone, but through the nervous system, the lived body, and the slow return to inner truth. Through private sessions, group work, and immersive journeys, she accompanies others as they meet fear with compassion, release old patterns, and learn to trust what is emerging from within.

She came to this work not by choosing it, but by being led to it. In the middle of her own imploding — a marriage ending, a career dissolving, a home being lost — a voice spoke to her that said, simply: *there is more to this life.* She didn't know what that meant. But she followed that curiosity. That path led her, unexpectedly, to shamanism — a world she had never encountered — and from there to teachers, elders, and sacred lands across the world who shaped her understanding of what it means to walk a threshold with honesty and care. For more than ten years, that curiosity has continued to guide both her life and her work.

A lifelong traveler and listener to place, Susan's path has been shaped by sacred landscapes — mountains, ancient stones, temples, rivers, and the quiet spaces where the earth speaks without words. These experiences, alongside her own thresholds of grief, awakening, and reinvention, inform the heart of her work.

She lives in San Diego, where she continues to walk her own edges, guide others through theirs, and listen for the truths that reveal themselves in the spaces between.

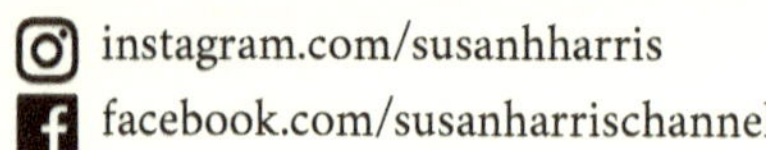

instagram.com/susanhharris
facebook.com/susanharrischannel

www.ingramcontent.com/pod-product-compliance
Lightning Source LLC
Chambersburg PA
CBHW031043160726
47991CB00005B/2009